Engaging Teachers, Students, and Families in K-6 Writing Instruction

This text draws on interviews, assignments, field notes, and observations from a flipped writing methodology course conducted with preservice elementary teachers in the US. In doing so, the text powerfully illustrates the benefits of using flipped methodologies in K-6 instruction to engage students, teachers, and families in authentic writing practices.

Engaging Teachers, Students, and Families in K-6 Writing Instruction demonstrates the use of flipped writing methodologies to engage preservice teachers in literacy instruction, increase their confidence as writers, and bolster their understanding and application of pedagogical content knowledge. In turn, this underpins teachers' ability to teach writing as an authentic, purpose-driven, audience-focused process. In particular, chapters explore effective teaching strategies including writing clinics, writing contests, and family literacy sessions which encourage writing development within a community of students, teachers, families, and authors.

This text will be an engaging and informative guide for educational researchers, teacher educators, and preservice and inservice teachers looking to develop effective flipped writing pedagogies to support educators, students, and families.

Danielle L. DeFauw is Associate Professor of Reading and Language Arts at the University of Michigan–Dearborn, USA.

Routledge Research in Literacy Education

This series provides cutting-edge research relating to the teaching and learning of literacy. Volumes provide coverage of a broad range of topics, theories, and issues from around the world, and contribute to developments in the field.

Recent titles in the series include:

Dialogic Literary Argumentation in High School Language Arts Classrooms
A Social Perspective for Teaching, Learning, and Reading Literature
David Bloome, George Newell, Alan Hirvela and Tzu-Jung Lin

Engaging Teachers, Students, and Families in K-6 Writing Instruction
Developing Effective Flipped Writing Pedagogies
Danielle L. DeFauw

For a complete list of titles in this series, please visit, https://www.routledge.com/Routledge-Research-in-Literacy-Education/book-series/RRLIT

Engaging Teachers, Students, and Families in K-6 Writing Instruction

Developing Effective Flipped Writing Pedagogies

Danielle L. DeFauw

NEW YORK AND LONDON

First published 2020
by Routledge
52 Vanderbilt Avenue, New York, NY 10017

and by Routledge
2 Park Square, Milton Park, Abingdon, Oxon, OX14 4RN

Routledge is an imprint of the Taylor & Francis Group, an informa business

© 2020 Taylor & Francis

The right of Danielle L. DeFauw to be identified as author of this work has been asserted by her in accordance with sections 77 and 78 of the Copyright, Designs and Patents Act 1988.

All rights reserved. No part of this book may be reprinted or reproduced or utilised in any form or by any electronic, mechanical, or other means, now known or hereafter invented, including photocopying and recording, or in any information storage or retrieval system, without permission in writing from the publishers.

Trademark notice: Product or corporate names may be trademarks or registered trademarks, and are used only for identification and explanation without intent to infringe.

Library of Congress Cataloging-in-Publication Data
Names: DeFauw, Danielle L., author.
Title: Engaging teachers, students, and families in K-6 writing instruction: developing effective flipped writing pedagogies/Danielle L. DeFauw.
Description: New York, NY: Routledge, 2021. | Series: Routledge research in literacy education | Includes bibliographical references and index. |
Identifiers: LCCN 2020013373 (print) | LCCN 2020013374 (ebook) | ISBN 9780367423940 (hardback) | ISBN 9780367823931 (ebook)
Subjects: LCSH: Composition (Language arts)–Study and teaching (Elementary) | Language arts (Elementary) | Flipped classrooms. | Home and school.
Classification: LCC LB1576 .D3137 2021 (print) | LCC LB1576 (ebook) | DDC 372.62/3–dc23
LC record available at https://lccn.loc.gov/2020013373
LC ebook record available at https://lccn.loc.gov/2020013374

ISBN: 978-0-367-42394-0 (hbk)
ISBN: 978-0-367-54015-9 (pbk)
ISBN: 978-0-367-82393-1 (ebk)

Typeset in Times New Roman
by Deanta Global Publishing Services, Chennai, India

To my greatest teacher of all, my heavenly Father, whose Word gives me strength and from Whom all blessings flow, and to the most special people He has blessed me to love: David, DeLainey, Dayana, and Drew.

Contents

List of Figure	ix
List of Tables	x
About the Author	xi
Acknowledgments	xii

Introduction: Preservice Teachers Unprepared to Teach Writing: I Hate Writing and You Want Me to Teach Students to Write? 1

PART I
Consuming Pedagogical Content Knowledge of Writing through Flipped Learning 19

1 Teacher Educators Use Flipped Learning: Writing Shoulder to Shoulder 21

2 Flipped Writing Methodology Course: Somersaulting through the Process 36

3 Writing Workshop: Writing for One Person to Make the Impossible Possible 48

PART II
Applying Pedagogical Content Knowledge of Writing through Academic Service Learning 63

4 Teach Writing: Connecting with Students and Families through Writing Clinics 65

viii *Contents*

5 Celebrate Writing: Connecting Students, Families, and Published Children's Book Authors and Illustrators through Writing Events 81

6 Evaluate Writing: Discovering Authentic Learning Opportunities through Writing Contests 92

PART III
Transferring Pedagogical Content Knowledge of Writing to Future Classrooms 103

7 Transfer Flipped Learning Opportunities: Building Home/School Connections Virtually 105

8 Transfer Writing Pedagogy: Becoming an Agent of Change in the Elementary Writing Classroom 118

Conclusion: Teach Writing 133

Appendix: Course Components 139
Index 149

Figure

0.1 Core Variables for Preservice Teacher Learning of
Pedagogical Content Knowledge of Writing 13

Tables

0.1	Research Study Participants' Demographic Details and Data Schedule	6
0.2	Original Data Coding	9
1.1	Academic Service Learning Context and Participants	26
2.1	Course Evaluations: Overall Assessment of the Course	41
4.1	Steps for Implementing Parent-Writer Groups	73
4.2	Books and Writing Prompts to Use with Families	74
5.1	2019 Young Authors' Festival Schedule	82
5.2	Courses' Organization for Young Authors' Festival	84
5.3	Examples of Breakout Session Topics	85
5.4	Afterschool Writing Event Schedule	88
A.1	Syllabus Example with In-Person Tasks, Online Modules, Required Readings, and Assignments	140
A.2	Flipped Writing Methodology Course Assignments	143
A.3	Flipped Writing Methodology Course Sample Lessons and Mentor Texts	147

About the Author

Danielle L. DeFauw, PhD, is Associate Professor of Reading and Language Arts in the Department of Education, Health, and Human Services at the University of Michigan–Dearborn. Dr. DeFauw's primary research interests focus on supporting teachers' development of their teacher-writer voices and use of authentic writing instruction to support students' writing growth. Authentic literacy contexts are central to her instructional and research interests focused on connecting students with published children's book authors, especially through author visits and writing festivals.

Acknowledgments

With sincerest gratitude I thank the research-study participants and all the preservice and inservice teachers I have been privileged to teach writing. We have learned so much together, especially through our community-based experiences. I thank all stakeholders involved in the community-based partnerships who have provided preservice teachers and children with myriad authentic learning opportunities. A special thank you to the Young Authors' Festival Committee and all the authors and illustrators who have joined our celebrations of literacy.

A special thank you to my editor, Ellie Wright, and her editorial team at Routledge for giving me this opportunity. Always, I will cherish our email exchanges, Ellie. Thank you, Barbara Kriigel, my dear friend, for volunteering to read and edit drafts of this book. Thank you to my colleagues and friends for your encouragement.

To my family who supported me throughout this writing process–with my whole heart–thank you! From helping with the kids to preparing meals to surprising me with gifts of time, so many of these words are written because of you.

DeLainey, Dayana, and Drew—You are such precious gifts and words cannot express how blessed I am to be your mom. Your hugs, laughter, and love fill me to tears. My prayer for you is that you will enjoy your life's journey. Trust God. Dream Big. Work hard. Be you.

And saving the best for last, thank you, David. I love you. I love our story.

Introduction
Preservice Teachers Unprepared to Teach Writing: I Hate Writing and You Want Me to Teach Students to Write?

Too many elementary inservice teachers are unprepared to teach K-6 writing methodology because too many preservice teacher education programs do not require a course focused on how to teach writing. As a former third-grade teacher and a teacher educator whose writing course was developed in 2013 and not required until 2017, I speak from varied experience.

Like many elementary preservice teachers earning their teaching certification, my university's teacher preparation program did not offer, let alone require, a course focused on K-6 writing methodology. Writing instruction was crammed into the reading methodology course. So as a new third-grade teacher on my first day of school, I scrawled a summer writing prompt across the whiteboard, familiar from my own apprenticeship experiences as an elementary school student (Lortie, 1975).

The morning bell rang and Devin (all names are pseudonyms) screamed, "I don't write!" He shoved his writer's notebook off his desk and slammed his blond head into his folded arms.

Slowly, I leaned down to pick up his writer's notebook, more so to hide from my students' shocked looks that mirrored my own. *What do I do with a student who hates to write, especially on the first day of school?* My heart pounded as I walked between the horseshoe-shaped rows. The only trick my brain captured stemmed from my early childhood education training: dictation.

I whispered, "Maybe you don't write, but I do. How about you tell me about your summer and I'll write it down."

Devin lifted his head and smashed his hand against his forehead. "Fine," he obliged. "But my summer sucked."

Devin shared details, and I wrote with increasing speed. When he finished talking, my handwriting filled two notebook pages.

Devin shrieked, "I wrote all that!"

That memory burned into my mind as I wondered, even in that moment, how in the world would I teach my students how to write, let alone motivate them to write?

Thankfully, the first moments with Devin turned out successful, but I questioned myself daily as teaching him and his classmates to write was riddled with challenges. As a third-grade teacher for eight years and a literacy specialist for three years, teaching writing challenged my colleagues and me. Motivated to make writing easier for elementary students, I independently studied, experienced, read, wrote, and participated in professional development opportunities to learn how to teach writing.

Just over a decade after my experience with Devin, I was tasked as a second-year assistant professor to prepare preservice teachers to teach writing. Despite three literacy degrees—a Bachelor's degree in Elementary Education with a Language Arts Major, a Master's degree in Literacy Specialization for K-12, and a Doctoral degree in Reading Education—I never took a writing methodology course. For my Master's degree and my Doctoral degree, I took a required writing course to develop my writerly voice. For my doctoral-program minor, my advisor and I created a writing minor; I completed independent studies to develop as a teacher-writer and wrote for professional purposes (Whitney et al., 2014), but my focus on how to teach my students how to write aside from modeling writing was limited. Research shows many teacher educators share similar experiences as many feel they are unprepared to teach teachers how to teach writing (Hodges et al., 2015; Myers et al., 2016).

I felt like a 1,000-piece puzzle emptied into my hands and I struggled to hold the pieces together: brainstorming, revision strategies, mentor texts, struggling writers, writing process, English Language Learner writers, teacher-writers, writing assessment, writing workshop, grammar, prewriting, spelling, conferencing, writing prompts, editing, and so many more. I began with a piece and then another until the image began to form. I wanted better for my preservice teachers than I experienced, but how would I find enough time to teach all the writing content and pedagogy my preservice teachers needed?

Teaching Writing Within Time Constraints

Kennedy (1998) argued reform-focused teacher education programs make a difference as they help ensure preservice teachers develop their ability to teach writing as an authentic, purpose-driven, audience-focused process versus a set of prescriptive rules inherent in traditional educator preparation programs. Kennedy stated many college courses either focus on writing content or pedagogy, but not both due to time constraints. With technological changes, elementary preservice teachers can apply pedagogical content knowledge within a single semester.

Shulman (1987) termed the phrase pedagogical content knowledge to signify the myriad content (theories, methods, facts) and pedagogical practices teachers need to blend within a discipline to teach students effectively:

> The key to distinguishing the knowledge base of teaching lies at the intersection of content and pedagogy, in the capacity of a teacher to transform the content knowledge he or she possesses into forms that are pedagogically powerful and yet adaptive to the variations in ability and background presented by the students.
>
> (p. 15)

Cochran et al. (1993) changed knowledge to knowing and defined pedagogical content knowing (PCKg) as "*a teacher's integrated understanding of four components of pedagogy, subject matter content, student characteristics, and the environmental context of learning*" (p. 266). Cochran et al. argued context is paramount to prospective teachers' pedagogical and content development.

With so many puzzle pieces, flipped learning (Talbert, 2017) provided the only way to teach all the necessary pedagogical content knowledge or knowing of writing:

> Flipped learning is a pedagogical approach in which direct instruction moves from the group learning space to the individual learning space, and the resulting group space is transformed into a dynamic, interactive learning environment where the educator guides students as they apply concepts and engage creatively in the subject matter.
>
> (Flipped Learning Network, 2014, n.p.)

Using flipped learning, I teach pedagogical content knowledge of writing (PCKW) to preservice teachers using direct-instruction modules available through our learning management system, Canvas. Through the course's 14-week curricular design, preservice teachers complete weekly online modules that include: (a) pre-recorded, topic-specific lectures; (b) assigned readings; (c) online discussions; (d) try-it tasks; and (e) independent writing. (See Appendix for module components.) Because preservice teachers learn online what traditionally would be their in-person lectures, time is available in-person to participate in writing workshop and professional learning communities (PLCs) (Dufour & Eker, 1998) focused on the academic service learning (ASL) projects.

In-person, twice a week, during the semester's first half, preservice teachers participated in writing workshop, a student-centered framework for teaching a classroom of students how to engage as a writing community through the writing process (Graves, 1983). Each writing workshop session consists of a mini lesson with modeling, think aloud, and study of mentor text(s); independent writing; one-on-one and small-group conferencing; and sharing. Preservice teachers develop their writing voices using the reciprocal writing process—prewriting, drafting, revising, editing, and publishing. During the semester's second half, within our regularly scheduled face-to-face class time (Tuesdays and Thursdays from 3:30 pm–4:45 pm), preservice teachers transfer their learning as writers to apply PCKW through three ASL opportunities: (a) tutor third-grade students in an afterschool writing clinic at a local urban elementary school; (b) evaluate writing contest entries submitted for the Young Authors' Festival (YAF) writing contest; and (c) lead breakout sessions and/or prepare virtual family resources for families attending the YAF. These ASL projects facilitate preservice teachers' authentic academic learning through community-based projects that meet the preservice teachers' and the community's needs (Howard, 1998). These components encompass the book's overall emphasis: a writing community is built through relationships with students, families, teachers, and published children's book authors. When preservice teachers experience such a writing community firsthand, they are more likely to transfer effective PCKW and connective experiences to their future classrooms (Shulman & Shulman, 2004), but such experiences need to be required within their educator preparation program.

Although some researchers have noted an increase in the number of studies exploring writing instruction for preservice teachers (Bomer et al., 2019), more empirical research is needed to explore elementary preservice teachers' preparation for teaching K-6 writing (Brenner & McQuirk, 2019; Morgan & Pytash, 2014; Myers et al., 2016); thus, I share this course's journey centered within the grounded theory study (Corbin & Strauss, 2014) conducted since 2014. Thus far, I have examined 27 elementary preservice teachers' experiences in the flipped writing methodology course, now a required course in the elementary education program at the University of Michigan–Dearborn (UM-D). UM-D is an urban, Midwest university of about 9,000 students with about 500 students in the Department of Education. I contemplate the following questions through lenses of sociocultural theory (Vygotsky & Cole, 1978; Wertsch, 1998), flipped learning (Abeysekera & Dawson, 2015), and the National Writing Project's (2020) tenets:

1. Through a flipped writing methodology course, how will preservice teachers develop their teacher-writer identity and writing abilities through writing workshop?
2. How will preservice teachers apply PCKW through ASL projects (e.g., third-grade writing clinic and YAF)?

Introduction 5

3. How will preservice teachers transfer their learning from their flipped writing methodology course to their future teaching experiences as preservice and inservice teachers?

Method

A grounded theory study was designed to explore answers to the research questions and develop new knowledge about how preservice teachers acquire their writing methodology repertoire and teacher-writer identity through a semester-long flipped writing methodology course.

Participants and Context

Per Internal Review Board approval, I invited preservice teachers who completed the flipped writing methodology course to participate in the research study once final grades posted. Due to the 27 undergraduate preservice teachers' course participation and choice to volunteer in the research, their data provided a convenient case for analyses (Merriam, 1998). See Table 0.1.

Data sources and Collection

Preservice teachers' data sources downloaded from Canvas included their field note journals with writing clinic lesson plans and reflections, writing history essays, writer's notebooks, informational/explanatory pieces, argument pieces, narrative pieces, peer feedback, try-it tasks/formative assessments and notes, eportfolio reflections, observations of two participants' student or inservice teaching, and transcribed post-course interviews. The standardized open-ended interviews included 13 semi-structured questions (Patton, 2015) adapted from Atwell (1998) and Street (2003):

1. How would you describe yourself as a writer?
2. How would you describe a positive/negative writing experience you have had (in or out of school)?
3. What is the easiest/hardest part of writing for you?
4. As you think of yourself working with students, helping them develop as writers, what do you see as your strengths/weaknesses?
5. How would you describe and how did you experience flipped learning/ the writing clinic/the writing contest evaluation process/the YAF?

Interviews were conducted either in my office on campus or virtually using BlueJeans video conferencing. Using preservice teachers' writing history essays (Morgan, 2010), I interviewed preservice teachers through an

Table 0.1 Research Study Participants' Demographic Details and Data Schedule

Pseudonym	Semester and Class	Ethnic Group	Interview	Observation
Carly	F '14 Senior	Arab American Female	2-16-15 (PRE) 12-14-15 (ST)	Declined
Serena	F '14 Senior	Arab American Female	2-12-15 (PRE)	Declined
Brenda	F '14 Senior	European American Female	2-16-15 (PRE) 12-14-15 (ST) 1-14-16 (IN) 1-31-17 (IN)	1-31-17 (IN)
Harper	F '14 Senior	European American Female	2-12-15 (PRE) 12-14-15 (ST)	Declined
Rhonda	F '14 Senior	European American Female	2-16-15 (PRE)	Declined
Jared	F '14 Senior	European American Male	2-12-15 (PRE) 11-2-16 (ST) 12-15-16 (ST) 1-31-17 (IN) 8-18-17 (IN)	11-4-16 (ST) 12-15-16 (ST)
Travis	F '14 Senior	European American Male	2-9-15 (PRE)	Declined
Ari	F '14 Cert-Only	European American Male	2-10-15 (PRE) 12-17-15 (ST)	Declined
Roberta	F '16 Senior	African American Female	2-9-17 (PRE)	Declined
Annie	F '16 Senior	European American Female	2-23-17 (PRE) 2-20-18 (ST)	Declined
Ryder	F '16 Freshman	European American Male	2-9-17 (PRE)	Current PRE
Deva	F '17 Senior	Arab American Female	2-8-18 (PRE)	*
Jowan Nabha (Anonymity Waived)	F '17 Junior	Arab American Female	2-9-18 (PRE)	Current PRE
Nadia	F '17 Sophomore	Arab American Female	5-22-18 (PRE)	*
Isla	F '17 Sophomore	Arab American Female	2-1-18 (PRE)	*
Andrea	F '17 Sophomore	European American Female	5-7-18 (PRE)	Changed Major

(*Continued*)

Table 0.1 Continued

Pseudonym	Semester and Class	Ethnic Group	Interview	Observation
Hannah	F '17 Junior	European American Female	5-8-18 (PRE)	Current PRE
Shannon	F '17 Sophomore	European American Female	2-9-18 (PRE)	Current PRE
Celeste	F '18 Sophomore	European American Female	2-19-19 (PRE)	Current PRE
Paula	F '18 Sophomore	European American Female	Declined	Current PRE
Renee	F '18 Sophomore	European American Female	Technology mishap	Current PRE
Megan	F '18 Junior	European American Female	10-10-19 (PRE)	Current PRE
Jacob	F '18 Cert Only	European American Male	5-23-19 (PRE)	*
Sana	F '19 Senior	Arab American Female	Declined	Current PRE
Maceo	F '19 Junior	Southeast Asian Male	Written	Current PRE
Jackie	F '19 Freshman	European American Female	1-22-20 (PRE)	Current PRE
Amber	F '19 Senior	European American Female	Declined	Current PRE

Note: PRE—Preservice Teacher, ST—Student Teacher, IN—Inservice Teacher, *—Field Placement Director Conflict of Interest; 21 females and 6 males: 1 African American, 7 Arab Americans, 18 European Americans, and 1 Southeast Asian

open-ended nature of questioning (Yin, 1994) to understand their experiences with writing.

The study design included observations of participants' writing instruction as student teachers and inservice teachers. Aside from Brenda and Jared, many participants did not invite me to observe their student or inservice teaching. Three participants—Annie, Ari, Carly, and Harper—invited me to interview them regarding their student teaching experiences and/or inservice teaching experiences. A conflict of interest became apparent when I accepted a promotion as Field Placement Director in May 2018; in this role, I work directly with student teachers and preservice teachers throughout their field experiences. Upon student teachers' graduation, I plan to interview participants regarding their student teaching and observe their inservice writing instruction.

Additionally, course artifacts were downloaded from Canvas: assignment descriptions and rubrics, syllabi, and lesson plans.

Data Analyses

Following each semester, grounded theory analyses of the data sources using NVivo included the constant comparative method as open, descriptive coding (Saldaña, 2013) and cross-case pattern and thematic analyses were used to inductively analyze (Patton, 2015) the data until saturation was evident (Corbin & Strauss, 2014). Throughout the data analyses, memos were written and saved electronically. First, I used open, descriptive coding to analyze all Word document data; this step required rereading, highlighting, and labeling data with descriptive codes. Coded data were sorted for the second round of axial coding, using cross-case pattern analyses (Patton, 2015).

From the five-year analyses, five prominent categories emerged: Transfer, Personal Choice, Identity, Motivation, and Assessment. See Table 0.2. Cross-case thematic analyses of the categories revealed the following three themes (Patton, 2015):

1. **Making writerly choices**: Preservice teachers felt motivated to write when provided personal choice, and they encouraged their students to make personal writing choices. For example, Isla connected her positive writing experience as a writer in the course to the importance of allowing choice for her future students:

   > A positive experience in school would definitely be when I get an opportunity to choose a topic … [and as a teacher] just give [students] their own choice of writing something and you'll find yourself impressed because if you force a topic on them that they don't know what they're saying, they might despise writing.

   (Isla, Post-Course Interview, February 1, 2018)

2. **Transferring as evidence and vision**: Preservice teachers implemented PCKW they experienced as writers to support students' writing

development through ASL projects. Preservice teachers anticipated using the PCKW in their future classrooms. For example, Carly shared the importance of modeling: "Modeling writing was a very important component of the course, which was mentioned a plethora of times during the semester. I plan to model writing with my students as much as possible in my class."

(Carly, Post-Course Interview, February 16, 2015)

3. **Identifying as a teacher-writer**: Preservice teachers did not identify as teacher-writers during the course. Preservice teachers felt they developed as writers and applied what they learned as they tutored students in writing, but a pronounced teacher-writer identity was not evident during the course aside from one example of a preservice teacher, Roberta, a published children's book author. She discussed her development as a teacher-writer in her eportfolio conclusion:

> The course field experiences afforded me opportunities to develop as a teacher-writer by enhancing my knowledge of strategies and tools to motivate students to write. My knowledge has had a reciprocal impact on the students that I work with in class and in the community.

Table 0.2 Original Data Coding

Category (No. of coded passages)	Category definition with prominent subcategories (No. of coded passages) and some subcategories' breakdown [No. of coded passages]
Transfer (594)	Preservice teachers transferred pedagogical content knowledge of writing from coursework to the writing clinic (420) and Young Authors' Festival (42) or their student teaching or inservice teaching contexts (80). They transferred teacher-writer strategies (52) either through action [28] or vision [24].
Personal Choice (158)	Preservice teachers used the writing process (41) for personal expression (31) and made writerly choices (86) regarding purpose [45], tool [24], topic [12], or audience [5].
Identity (107)	Preservice teachers demonstrated characteristics of or offered phrases related to writer-identity (58), teacher of writing identity (36), or teacher-writer identity (13).
Assessment (99)	Preservice teachers addressed assessment as feedback (43) or conferencing (30) or high-stakes test preparation (26) for formative or evaluative purposes.
Motivation (96)	Preservice teachers connected with writers' (students' or peers') struggles (52). They focused on their own and their students' interests (32) or audiences (12).

To verify the data, I (a) used member checking of interview accuracies, (b) triangulated data sources, and (c) clarified my questions and biases as the researcher through reflexive journaling (Corbin & Strauss, 2014).

Findings

This grounded theory study's findings are organized around the three themes that emerged through open and axial coding. Preservice teachers' quotes from post-course interviews and documents provide additional illustration. Selective coding supported the theoretical conceptualization.

Making Writerly Choices

Evidence reveals preservice teachers felt motivated to write for teachers who honored their writing choices. Preservice teachers enjoyed self-expression through personal topic choice, purpose, and tools. Certain tools (e.g., writer's notebooks, blank hardcover books used for the writing clinic) made the writing products authentic. Preservice teachers highlighted experiences when they were allowed to write for audiences they cared about within chosen genres. Such positive personal writing experiences motivated preservice teachers to encourage students' writing choices. For example, Jared and Carly encouraged their students to write about their favorite topics, cats and candy sushi, respectively.

On the contrary, although Ari highlighted in his writing history essay his desire for topic choice in his own writing, he did not honor a student's choice during the writing clinic per his field note journal:

> He was quite enthusiastic to express his interests in science, but more so in the realm of science fiction. Discussions about time machines came up and I had to relay to my student that time machines are not real, even though there are some science concepts behind such machines. Eventually the discussion veered towards plants and how they grow. I found this to be a perfect and acceptable book to write about since my student was able to give me several details about how a plant grows.

Since I encouraged preservice teachers to support students' nonfiction writing development, Ari may not have considered science fiction an option. Pressure to meet course requirements may have overpowered his willingness to permit topic choice. Data showed participants felt pressure to ensure their students complete a final copy for the writing clinic celebration.

I remember becoming a little frustrated when we're halfway through and she changed her topic. And just becoming distracted when I knew myself that we had a deadline to meet.

(Hannah, Post-Course Interview, May 8, 2018)

Transferring as Evidence and Vision

Evidence revealed preservice teachers supported students' writing development through PCKW that preservice teachers experienced firsthand as writers. The writing clinic provided preservice teachers extended time to transfer their personal writing experiences to pedagogical practices. Field note journal entries included lesson plans and reflections, which demonstrated evidence of course-content transfer. For example, Jared's lesson objective stated, "Students will be able to list topics of non-fiction they find interesting. They will begin brainstorming ideas." A step in his procedure stated, "Give the students 3 minutes to write about each topic." Jared wrote authority lists during our in-class writing workshop sessions as I modeled. Authority lists include topics a writer feels knowledgeable about per individual experience (Atwell, 1998). His lesson plan did not include a step for modeling, but in his reflection, he stated, "I modeled an authority list … and then shared my ideas. [My student] then created her list, and she mentioned so many things about her cats."

Similarly, Jared's YAF lesson plan stated the following steps:

> Some of the teachers will listen to a song, model the process of drawing and writing on a large whiteboard for all to see, and then explain their way of thinking to the entire group.

Jared's example illustrates how preservice teachers implement teacher-writer pedagogy (Locke, 2015), especially using their own writing as mentor texts, or texts they hope students will emulate in their own writing (Dorfman & Cappelli, 2009), even though they did not self-identify as teacher-writers.

Identifying as a Teacher-Writer

Interestingly, despite my choice words consistently referencing the preservice teachers as teacher-writers (Johnston, 2004), the evidence revealed the term teacher-writer in only five preservice teachers' data:

1. Roberta is a published children's book author;

2. Jackie completed the teacher-writer module and the writing history essay simultaneously and mentioned teacher-writer again in her eportfolio (detailed below);
3. Jowan Nabha (anonymity waived) used the term teacher-writer in her eportfolio;
4. Isla used the term *student*-teacher-writer in her eportfolio; and
5. Paula mentioned being a student-writer while learning to be a teacher-writer in her eportfolio.

Jackie's following eportfolio quote illustrates the transgression a teacher-writer identity may require:

> I am already starting to understand the importance of being a teacher-writer and its influence on students. As an aspiring elementary teacher, I am excited to learn how to become a teacher-writer and possibly someone that just overall enjoys writing.

Preservice teachers identify themselves as writers, but not as teacher-writers. Perhaps identifying as a teacher-writer is not imperative (Brooks, 2007) or perhaps such an identity requires professional development. Additionally, through reflexive journaling, I realized my bias regarding the teacher-writer identity.

I identify as a teacher-writer. Personally, I have a natural disposition for writing. Although a love for reading motivates many educators to pursue the English Language Arts, writing has always been my passion (Cremin & Locke, 2017). Professionally, I believe teachers who choose to write anticipate their students' writing challenges (Graves, 1983). I also believe claiming a teacher-writer identity propels teachers to publish pieces that represent true experiences within their educational contexts (Whitney, 2009). I believe teachers need to use their educator voices to impact change throughout their careers (Whitney, 2017). Throughout the course implementation process, I envision the preservice teachers enacting teacher-writer identities as preservice and inservice teachers.

In one instance, Jowan Nabha identified herself as a "beginner writer, not an experienced writer," but she demonstrated teacher-writer aspirations when she sought publication for her argument piece. Additionally, she discovered the #TeachWrite blog and published a few blog posts. Most recently, she shared a draft chapter of a young adult novel she aims to finish. Jowan's experiences showcase her teacher-writer development yet she did not self-identify as a teacher-writer during the course.

The preservice teachers may have disregarded self-identification as a teacher-writer and instead focused on developing their own writing abilities while overcoming past perceptions of writing instruction (Hall & Grisham-Brown, 2011). Upon further reflection, however, I understood preservice teachers do not identify as teachers. The identification as a teacher-writer requires, at minimum, three levels of identification: writer, teacher, and teacher-writer. Developmentally, preservice teachers may not be ready to claim the teacher-writer identity.

Theoretical Conceptualization

The objective of any grounded theory study is to provide a theoretical conceptualization of the core categories' themes. For this study, the interconnectedness between making choices, transferring as evidence and vision, and identifying as teacher-writers is diagrammed in Figure 0.1.

Selective coding of the three themes' properties revealed a theoretical understanding that preservice teachers learn writing content as they explore their own writing development, make choices in their writing, and write for audiences they care about personally and professionally. The teacher-writer identity is not necessary for preservice teachers to transfer PCKW they apply through field experience opportunities. As preservice teachers reflect, they anticipate the PCKW they look forward to implementing as student and inservice teachers as the following quote illustrates:

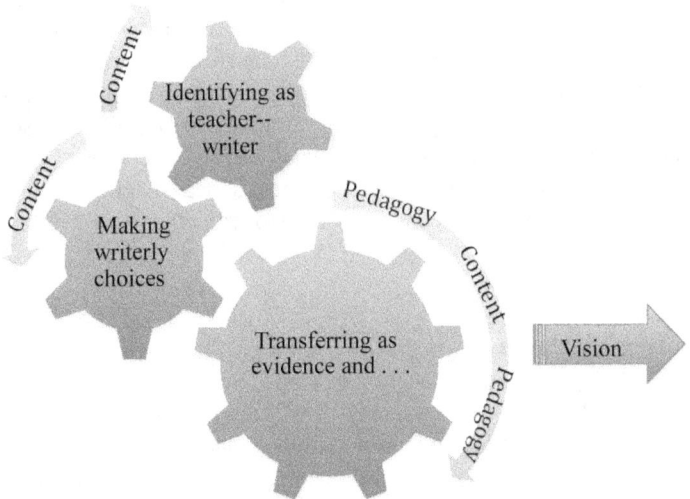

Figure 0.1 Core Variables for Preservice Teacher Learning of Pedagogical Content Knowledge of Writing.

I am going to use what I have learned and my experiences in this class to shape my future writing instruction. I want to encourage my students to write and to enjoy writing. I want to incorporate writing into every subject, as we should, and I want them to be motivated to write authentic pieces they are proud of. Nothing would make me happier than to inspire … my students to grow in the ways I have this semester and to look at writing not as a boring necessity but as an enjoyable activity used to accentuate personal growth.

(Harper, Post-Course Interview, February 12, 2015)

Using flipped learning, preservice teachers did not self-identify as teacher-writers, but they did develop their teaching repertoire concerning PCKW. Preservice teachers' understanding of how to write transferred to their pedagogical knowledge of how to teach elementary students to write. They learned within an authentic learning context that high-quality writing instruction is challenging to implement, but with dedicated practice and deep reflection, such instruction supports all writers in their development—the students and themselves.

Limitations

Limitations are inherent in every study. Generalizability is a limitation of this study as the grounded theory may not transfer to other contexts (Patton, 2015). Also, as the professor of the course and as the "analytic tool" of this research study, I had to consistently reflect on how my biases regarding what I hoped students would learn fogged the evidence collected (American Psychological Association, 2020, p. 17). Through memo writing, member checking, and reflexive journaling (Corbin & Strauss, 2014), I aimed to see what the evidence thoroughly revealed, especially in the interviews where preservice teachers may have told me what I wanted to hear. Triangulation of the data helped ensure interview comments aligned with other data.

The Journey Begins

Throughout this book's three sections—Consuming PCKW through Flipped Learning, Applying PCKW through Academic Service Learning, and Transferring PCKW to Future Classrooms—I will discuss the grounded theory supported by the empirical evidence the preservice teachers' interview quotes, assignments, and observations provided. In Chapter 1, I highlight the literature surrounding flipped learning and academic service learning used as the basis for the flipped writing methodology course design. In Chapter 2, I build upon the literature review to detail how teacher educators flip their writing courses for preservice teachers to support transfer of PCKW to elementary classrooms. In Chapter 3, I highlight writing workshop instruction for in-person sessions where preservice teachers develop their teacher-writer voices as they write for specific audiences and authentic publication.

Throughout the flipped writing methodology course, preservice teachers apply writing pedagogy through ASL opportunities, as Part II highlights. I suggest coupling PLCs and ASL projects as flipped learning creates space during in-person sessions for PLCs to focus on ASL preparation. The first ASL project details the afterschool writing clinic, detailed in Chapter 4. Included are steps for implementing a university or school-based writing clinic to celebrate literacy with families and connect families with published children's book authors. Chapter 5 highlights the second ASL project, the YAF, which includes multiple authentic learning opportunities: a literacy event, a writing contest, and virtual family resources. In Chapter 6, I detail writing assessment and how writing contests may provide students with an authentic opportunity for high-stakes writing assessment preparation. Writing contests also provide an evaluation opportunity for preservice teachers.

Part III explores how to transfer writing pedagogy to future classrooms. Chapter 7 includes suggestions for teaching preservice teachers how to flip writing workshop content through family resources they create to build home/school connections. Chapter 8 conceptualizes the grounded theory as preservice teachers demonstrate a "becoming" of teacher-writers growing in their ability to transfer PCKW. The Conclusion highlights the need for required writing methodology courses in higher education.

References

Abeysekera, L., & Dawson, P. (2015). Motivation and cognitive load in the flipped classroom: Definition, rationale and a call for research. *Higher Education Research and Development, 34*(1), 1–14. doi:10.1080/07294360.2014.934336

American Psychological Association. (2020). *Publication manual of the American Psychological Association* (7th ed.). doi:10.1037/0000165-000

Atwell, N. (1998). *In the middle: New understandings about writing, reading, and learning.* Boynton/Cook Publishers, Inc.

Bomer, R., Land, C.L., Rubin, J.C., & Van Dike, L.M. (2019). Constructs of teaching writing in research about literacy teacher education. *Journal of Literacy Research, 51*(2), 196–213. doi:10.1177/1086296X19833783

Brenner, D., & McQuirk, A. (2019). A snapshot of writing in elementary teacher preparation programs. *The New Educator, 15*(1), 18–29. doi:10.1080/1547688X.2018.1427291

Brooks, G.W. (2007). Teachers as readers and writers and as teachers of reading and writing. *Journal of Educational Research, 100*(3), 177–191. doi:10.3200/JOER.100.3.177-191

Cochran, K.F., DeRuiter, J.A., & King, R.A. (1993). Pedagogical content knowing: An integrative model for teacher preparation. *Journal of Teacher Education, 44*(4), 263–272.

Corbin, J., & Strauss, A. (2014). *Basics of qualitative research: Techniques and procedures for developing grounded theory* (4th ed.). SAGE Publications, Inc.

Cremin, T., & Locke, T. (Eds.). (2017). Introduction. In *Writer identity and the teaching and learning of writing* (pp. xvii–xxxi). Routledge. doi:10.4324/9781315669373

Dorfman, L.R., & Cappelli, R. (2009). *Nonfiction mentor texts: Teaching informational writing through children's literature K-6*. Stenhouse Publishers.

DuFour, R., & Eker, R. (1998). *Professional learning communities at work: Best practices for enhancing student achievement*. Solution Tree Press.

Flipped Learning Network. (2014). *What is flipped learning?* http://flippedlearning.org/wp-content/uploads/2016/07/FLIP_handout_FNL_Web.pdf

Graves, D.H. (1983). *Writing: Teachers & children at work*. Heinemann.

Hall, A.H., & Grisham-Brown, J. (2011). Writing development over time: Examining preservice teachers' attitudes and beliefs about writing. *Journal of Early Childhood Teacher Education, 32*(2), 148–158. doi:10.1080/10901027.20111.572230

Hodges, T.S., McTigue, E.M., Jareds, A.G., Weber, N.D., Wright, K.L., & De La Garza, A. (2015). Modeling the "write" teaching practices: Instructor influences on preservice teachers. In Y. Li & J. Hammer (Eds.), *Teaching at work* (pp. 143–167). Sense Publishers.

Howard, J.P.F. (1998). Academic service learning: A counternormative pedagogy. *New Direction for Teaching and Learning, 73*, 21–29. doi:10.1002/tl.7303

Johnston, P.H. (2004). *Choice words: How our language affects children's learning*. Stenhouse Publishers.

Kennedy, M.M. (1998). *Learning to teach writing: Does teacher education make a difference?* Teachers College Press.

Locke, T. (2015). *Developing writing teachers: Practical ways for writers to transform their classroom practice*. Routledge. doi:10.4324/9780203096451

Lortie, D.C. (1975). *Schoolteacher: A sociological study*. University of Chicago Press. https://www.press.uchicago.edu/ucp/books/book/chicago/S/bo3645184.html

Merriam, S.B. (1998). *Qualitative research and case study applications in education* (2nd ed.). Jossey-Bass.

Morgan, D. (2010). Preservice teachers as writers. *Literacy Research and Instruction, 49*(4), 352–365. doi:10.1080/19388070903296411

Morgan, D.N., & Pytash, K.E. (2014). Preparing preservice teachers to become teachers of writing: A 20-year review of the research literature. *English Education, 47*(1), 6–37.

Myers, J., Scales, R.Q., Grisham, D.L., Wolsey, T.D., Dismuke, S., Smetana, L., Yoder, K.K., Ikpeze, C., Ganske, K., & Martin, S. (2016). What about writing? A national exploratory study of writing instruction in teacher preparation programs. *Literacy Research and Instruction, 55*(4), 309–330. doi:10.1080/19388071.2016.1198442

National Writing Project. (2020). *What we do*. https://www.nwp.org/what-we-do

Patton, M.Q. (2015). *Qualitative research & evaluation methods*. Sage Publications.

Saldaña, J. (2013). *The coding manual for qualitative researchers*. Sage Publications.
Shulman, L.S. (1987). Knowledge and teaching: Foundations of the new reform. *Harvard Educational Review*, *57*(1), 1–23. doi:10.17763/haer.57.1.j463w79r56455411
Shulman, L.S., & Shulman, J.H. (2004). How and what teachers learn: A shifting perspective. *Journal of Curriculum Studies*, *36*(2), 257–271. doi:10.1177/0022057409189001-202
Street, C. (2003). Preservice teachers' attitudes about writing and learning to teach writing: Implications for teacher educators. *Teacher Education Quarterly*, *30*(3), 33–50.
Talbert, R. (2017). *Flipped learning: A guide for higher education faculty*. Stylus Publishing.
Vygotsky, L.S., & Cole, M. (1978). *Mind in society: The development of higher psychological processes*. Harvard University Press. doi:10.2307/j.ctvjf9vz4
Wertsch, J.V. (1998). *Mind as action*. Oxford University Press. doi:10.1093/acprof:oso/9780195117530.001.0001
Whitney, A. (2009). Writer, teacher, person: Tensions between personal and professional writing in a National Writing Project summer institute. *English Education*, *41*(3), 236–259.
Whitney, A. (2017). Developing the teacher-writer in professional development. In T. Cremin & T. Locke (Eds.), *Writer identity and the teaching and learning of writing* (pp. 67–80). Routledge. doi:10.4324/9781315669373
Whitney, A.E., Zuidema, L.A., & Fredricksen, J.E. (2014). Understanding teachers' writing: Authority in talk and texts. *Teachers and Teaching: Theory and Practice*, *20*(1), 59–73. doi:10.1080/13540602.2013.848515
Yin, R.K. (1994). *Case study research: Design and methods* (2nd ed.). Sage Publications.

Part I
Consuming Pedagogical Content Knowledge of Writing through Flipped Learning

1 Teacher Educators Use Flipped Learning

Writing Shoulder to Shoulder

Inherent power exists in writing and, as teacher educators, we must ensure every child can fully experience writing's power. I argue we must support preservice teachers first if we want to see a change in elementary students' writing. The most current US landscape of students' writing assessments from the National Assessment of Education, completed in 2002, reveals only 28% of fourth-grade students demonstrate writing proficiency (NAEP, n.d.). Perhaps data collected in 2017 provides stronger results, but NAEP (2019) stated "grades 4 and 8 revealed potentially confounding factors in measuring performance" (n.p.). The NAEP will address these factors in a special report Summer 2020. Teaching K-6 writing is a complex process; thus, preservice teachers need thorough preparation and must be required to take a writing methodology course (Martin & Dismuke, 2015; Zimmerman et al., 2014).

Recently, Myers et al. (2019) highlighted 15 writing teacher educators' experiences connecting their writing methodology courses with K-12 field experiences; 11 of the writing teacher educators taught elementary preservice teachers. I hope you were required to take such a writing methodology course as a preservice teacher and that you teach a required writing methodology course as a teacher educator. But for too many of us, writing instruction is enfolded in literacy courses that emphasize reading (Collier et al., 2015; Lenski et al., 2013; Stockinger, 2007). Brenner and McQuirk (2019) reviewed 155 required literacy courses from 42 teacher preparation programs across 7 states in the US and discovered only 2 preparation programs required courses specific to writing pedagogy while 70 focused on reading, 59 focused on the English language arts, and 24 focused on children's literature. Granted, of the 59 required courses focused on the English language arts, writing was likely addressed, but course descriptions targeted reading. Spiker (2015) stated, "My course focus was predominantly on how to teach reading. Writing was a topic left for stolen time at the end of the semester" (p. 35).

Stolen time will never provide preservice teachers the breadth of experience and depth of knowledge they need to understand the pedagogical content knowledge of writing (PCKW) their future elementary students will need (ILA & NCTE, 2017; Shulman, 1987). Even if a writing course is required of elementary preservice teachers, Kennedy (1998) argued most semester-long courses focus on content or pedagogy, not both. Time is too scarce to teach preservice teachers how to write and how to teach writing (Kennedy, 1998); however, two decades later with new technologies available, teacher educators can prepare preservice teachers to know and apply both content and pedagogy.

To meet my preservice teachers' needs, I designed a course using flipped learning to ensure the preservice teachers I have the opportunity to teach are prepared within a semester timeframe. This course design became the catalyst for the grounded theory I developed as analysis of the preservice teachers' learning revealed the interconnectedness between their development as writers, the application of writing pedagogy as preservice teachers, and anticipation of their future elementary students' needs regarding writing instruction.

Throughout this chapter, I will connect the research literature to show how I teach writing within a sociocultural theoretical lens to help teacher-writers develop their own personal writing voices through writing workshop. Our in-person writing workshop sessions follow the National Writing Project's (2020) tenets. Because there is so much content and pedagogy to teach, I used flipped learning to teach preservice teachers the writing content outside of class through our learning management system, Canvas. In-person, preservice teachers experience pedagogical knowledge and transfer their learning of PCKW to academic service learning (ASL) experiences where they provide elementary students with authentic writing instruction.

Theoretical Orientation

The theoretical orientation for this research is multifaceted: sociocultural theory, the National Writing Project's tenets, and flipped learning. Sociocultural theory provides a foundation for exploring writers' experiences within communities of practice (Lave & Wenger, 1991; Wenger et al., 2002) such as classroom writing communities where writers engage in "sociocognitive apprenticeships" (Englert et al., 2006, p. 209). Sociocognitive apprenticeship conceptualizes how teachers model their own writing process for students through think alouds (Atwell, 1998). Like their teachers, students need to learn to write for authentic purposes through real-life contexts (Herrington & Herrington, 2006) using the reciprocal writing process (rehearsing, drafting, revising, and presenting) to communicate socially with varied audiences (Flower & Hayes, 1981, 1984). Authentic purposes are addressed through the writing workshop framework (mini lesson, independent writing, conferencing, and sharing) (Graves, 1983). Active engagement in such communities of practice as writing workshop and ASL projects (Bringle & Hatcher, 1996) promotes authentic learning (Herrington & Herrington, 2006).

As preservice teachers participate in authentic learning throughout their personal writing processes in writing workshop, they develop their writerly voices (Whyte et al., 2007). As the professor, I model how to implement writing workshop as a teacher-writer. As a teacher-writer, I choose to transfer what I understand about my own writing process to my teaching contexts (Cremin & Myhill, 2012). "The 'Teachers as Writers' movement ... [contends] that when teachers embrace the identity of writer, their practices as teachers of writing undergo a transformation that enhances the experience of writing and writing performance of their students" (Locke, 2015, n.p.). Teacher-writers transfer their personal writing workshop experiences to facilitate their students' writing development in various contexts (Cremin & Myhill, 2012). Teacher-writers model writing and conduct think alouds (Atwell, 1998) to support students' writing development and self-efficacy (Pajares & Valiante, 2006).

Because preservice teachers also need to develop their self-efficacy in their teaching abilities, the course aligns to flipped learning pedagogy to create space for social, active learning in writing workshop and ASL projects during in-class time while traditional lecture content is delivered online, outside of class (e.g., Abeysekera & Dawson, 2015; Hoffman, 2014; Moffett, 2015). The Flipped Learning Network (2014) specifies differences between Flipped Learning and Flipped Classrooms: "Flipping a class can, but does not necessarily, lead to Flipped Learning" (p. 1). To achieve flipped learning, teachers must implement student-centered instruction, expect self-reflection, differentiate, provide feedback, ensure transfer of learning between online and in-class content, and formatively assess students' learning (Flipped Learning Network, 2014).

Flipped Learning in Writing Courses

In an upper-level, English, higher-education course, Brooks (2014) explored sophomores' informational literacy skills. Students who participated in six, short online videos and attended one face-to-face session detailing informational literacy skills used more peer-reviewed journal articles in their final research papers than students who only participated in the one face-to-face informational library session. Zhonggen and Guifang (2016) studied undergraduate students' satisfaction and academic achievement within a flipped business English writing course. The professor used clickers to formatively assess students' online learning during in-class sessions. Instant results determined the professor's next instructional steps. Webb and Doman (2016) reported 64 students' grammar improvement in English as a Foreign Language and English as a Second Language course due to flipped learning pedagogy.

Other researchers have flipped composition courses. Beckelhimer (2015) required students to choose screencasting software to portray their research processes: keyword searches, annotated bibliographies, and source analyses. Using the flipped learning course design allowed Beckelhimer to support students' writing processes efficiently. Grimsley (2015) taught a hybrid composition course. She provided 19 students with 10 video podcasts, 3 of which were optional, and 4 in-person sessions. Unfortunately, over half of the students did not watch the 7 required podcasts. The three optional podcasts were not viewed by any students. Surprisingly, students provided positive survey responses concerning the video podcasts and in-person course sessions. Not surprisingly, students learned content if they participated in the flipped learning components. Prodoehl (2015) highlighted four professors' online-module use designed to support students' argument writing skills. The faculty supported students' idea generation, revision, and argument analysis through modules. Students applied their learning in and outside of class. The modules facilitated students' writing preparation for in-person writing conferences with faculty.

The literature highlights three studies that align closest to the flipped writing methodology course design highlighted in this book. First, Crisafulli (2015) reported five semesters of a flipped composition course with freshmen and sophomores. Through redesigned video content, student participation increased. Students learned argument writing techniques they transferred to in-class workshop sessions where they demonstrated writing improvement. Second, Buitrago and Diaz (2016) flipped an English course for 32 students learning English as a Foreign Language in Colombia. In-class time included writing compare/contrast essays rather than grammar instruction. Diaz formatively assessed grammar with Kahoot! quizzes to ascertain students' content understanding they acquired from at-home videos. Buitrago's and Diaz's pilot study revealed students' writing development improved with: (a) completing five, at-home writing workshop lessons, two focused on compare/contrast essay structure; and (b) using class time to write and receive feedback during the writing process. Third, Rochester et al. (2018) highlighted a literacy methods course for K-2 preservice teachers that utilized flipped learning to support their in- and outside-of-class experiential learning. Preservice teachers found flipped learning beneficial as demonstrated through surveys and field experiences, because the lectures and videos they viewed outside of class prepared them well for the in-class discussions, observations, and application of K-2 pedagogy.

Through my flipped writing methodology course, I teach preservice teachers PCKW they need to transfer to field experiences, student teaching, and their future elementary classrooms (Myers et al., 2019). Through the flipped learning course design, preservice teachers experience PCKW as they participate in writing workshop during the semester's first half; I model how to run a writing workshop while supporting their writing development in informational/explanatory and argument genres. Also, preservice teachers acquire PCKW outside of class throughout the semester. During the semester's second half, preservice teachers apply PCKW in class through ASL projects.

Academic Service Learning

Teacher education institutions should partner with schools to support preservice teachers' pedagogical development and students' writing development through ASL opportunities (Bringle & Hatcher, 1996; Hart, 2007). In the next chapter, I will highlight how to implement the various flipped learning components to create space for ASL opportunities. My messy journey with ASL opportunities evolved over the last five years as Table 1.1 demonstrates and the following section describes.

First Session (Not Flipped)

In 2012, I designed the course *EXPS 498/598: Exploring Writing with Children & Adolescents*, described as follows:

> This course provides a theoretical foundation for writing instruction for children in grades K-6. Emphasis is placed on modeling, instructional strategies, and assessment for supporting student writers that teachers use to facilitate children's development of written language. Focus will be on the development of children's writing abilities and the ways in which this development is fostered throughout the primary, intermediate, and middle grades.

Just prior to designing the course, I created a ten-hour online professional development writing course for inservice teachers, which I included in the course. Just prior to this, I had completed my experience as an ASL fellow through the University of Michigan–Dearborn, and I designed the course to receive ASL designation. ASL designation allowed me an opportunity to create a free, third-grade, university writing clinic offered during our course timeframe in the semester's second half.

Initially, Winter 2013 EXPS 498/598 ran with three preservice and two inservice teachers. During our weekly Tuesday sessions from 6:00 pm to

Table 1.1 Academic Service Learning Context and Participants

Semester	Writing Clinic	Writing Clinic Participants	Young Authors' Festival	Contest Evaluation
Winter 2013 3 undergraduates and 2 graduates Not Flipped Not Required	6 University sessions (6:15–7:30 pm)	10 female students: 8 African American, 1 European American, 1 Mexican American	No	No
Fall 2014 21 undergraduates and 4 graduates Flipped Not Required	6 Urban A Elementary sessions (6:15–7:30 pm)	16 students: 8 female, 8 male; 12 African American, 2 European American, 2 Latino/Hispanic	Two 20-minute sessions	141 entries: 3rd (33), 4th (86), 5th (22)
Fall 2016 8 undergraduates Flipped Required for elementary PSTs Reading major/minors	Urban B Elementary canceled; 10 University sessions (3:45–4:45 pm)	24 students: 15 female, 9 male; 4 African American, 11 Arab American, 6 European American, 3 Latino/Hispanic	Two 50-minute sessions	259 entries: 3rd (52), 4th (59), 5th (148)
Fall 2017 21 undergraduates Flipped Required for all elementary preservice teachers	7 Urban C Elementary sessions (3:45–4:45 pm)	16 students: 8 female, 8 male; 3 African American, 4 Arab American, 4 European American, 1 Latino/Hispanic	Same as F '16	116 entries: 3rd (17), 4th (39), 5th (60)

(*Continued*)

Table 1.1 Continued

Semester	Writing Clinic	Writing Clinic Participants	Young Authors' Festival	Contest Evaluation
Fall 2018 24 undergraduates Same as F '17	5 Urban C Elementary sessions (3:45–4:45 pm)	25 students: 12 female, 13 male; 3 African American, 20 Arab American, 2 European American	Parent Poster (10-minute sessions) No breakout session Flipped Parent Resource	72 entries: 3rd (5), 4th (35), 5th (32)
Fall 2019 20 undergraduates Same as F '17	5 Urban C Elementary sessions (3:45–4:45 pm)	36 students: 22 female, 14 male; 3 African American, 21 Arab American, 9 European American, 3 Latino/Hispanic	Same as F '18	128 entries: 3rd (2), 4th (25), 5th (101)

8:45 pm, I led the preservice and inservice teachers through an hour-long writing workshop: mini lesson, independent writing with conferencing, and sharing. I required them to write three pieces—narrative, poetry, informational/explanatory—for specific audiences they chose, based on mentor texts. Unfortunately, the preservice and inservice teachers completed most writing outside of class because I often cut into writing workshop with traditional lecture to ensure they understood the PCKW they needed to implement with third-grade students enrolled in the university writing clinic.

Like Hawkins et al. (2019), I expected preservice and inservice teachers to teach in their field experience, the writing clinic, the way I modeled for them during our writing workshop sessions: using mentor texts, modeling with their own writing, conducting think alouds, and encouraging their students to write. While the preservice teachers tutored the ten third-grade students who attended six, one-hour-and-fifteen-minute sessions, I met with the families to discuss home/school literacy support (DeFauw, 2017). During the final session, the students read aloud their writing to their families as we celebrated literacy.

After each session, the preservice teachers collaborated during the last hour to design a four-week, grade-level specific, nonfiction, unit-of-study (Morgan, 2010). Although preservice teachers learned content and one inservice teacher published her narrative (DeFauw & Smith, 2016), the course felt crammed. I needed more time to teach, but time was scarce.

Second Session (Flipped)

For Fall 2014, EXPS 498/598 ran with 21 preservice and 4 inservice early childhood teachers whose constructivist course was canceled. The writing methodology course was used to fulfill the program requirement. The course description remained the same, but I needed to make the same course components more manageable. Serendipitously, I found the Flipped Learning Network (2014) online at flippedlearning.org. Suddenly, I knew how I could ensure my preservice teachers received the: (a) lectures needed to develop their PCKW, while developing their teacher-writer voices through writing workshop; and (b) writing pedagogy they experienced, learned, and transferred to the third-grade writing clinic and Young Authors' Festival (YAF).

During the semester's second half, six tutoring sessions were held at a local elementary school (to ease transportation challenges for families) from 6:15 pm–7:30 pm on Tuesdays. The K-6 urban elementary school served 840 students, of which 69.5% were African American, 22% were European American, 4.5% were Latino/Hispanic, 3% were two or more races, 0.5% were Asian, and 0.5% were American Indian or Alaskan Native. As a Title I school, 73% received free/reduced lunch. This school was one of two elementary schools in a district that included 1 middle school, and 2 high schools, serving 2,300 students overall. This ASL project, connected directly to the course's learning goals, provided a meaningful service to the elementary school (Howard, 1998).

Preservice and inservice teachers tutored their students while I met with families to discuss home/school literacy connections. All learners (elementary students and families) were supported to develop their writer's craft, demonstrate confidence in their writing ability, use mentor texts to emulate in their own fiction and nonfiction writing, and acquire multiple strategies to transfer their learning of writer's craft between genres and contexts. Following the first five tutoring sessions, the preservice and inservice teachers formed professional learning communities (PLCs) of three to four preservice or inservice teachers to discuss their plans for the next session and debrief with me at the elementary school. The sixth writing clinic session encompassed the entire course timeframe to celebrate the families' participation in the writing clinic. Award-winning author/illustrator, Matt Faulkner, shared his passion for writing and illustrating children's books with the audience. Students shared their final writing with the audience alongside their tutors. Even though the six sessions were riddled with attendance challenges, the preservice teachers applied their PCKW and found the writing clinic beneficial. "As an educator, I know the little time we had made a difference. I can only imagine what a whole school year can do" (Serena, Post-Course Interview, February 12, 2015).

An additional ASL project—the YAF, which is a free half-day event for third- through fifth-grade students and their families to celebrate literacy—was added to provide preservice teachers opportunities to assess writing and interact with families (DeFauw et al., 2017). The YAF, originally designed to support the University's mission and coupled with the children's literature course I teach, provided a valuable outlet for preservice teachers in the writing course to evaluate third- through fifth-grade students' writing contest entries. Preservice teachers used a holistic rubric we created based on published examples to determine the winners. Additionally, the preservice teachers led two instructional sessions (content repeated) for the students. The YAF also created an opportunity for the preservice teachers to connect with families and the YAF's honorarium, published children's book author, Toni Buzzeo. She shared her experience writing, publishing, and celebrating the Caldecott Award her book, *One Cool Friend*, won to honor David Small's illustrations.

Third Session

For Fall 2016, the course achieved permanent placement in the university's preservice, elementary, educator preparation program for preservice teachers earning reading majors and minors. The course also received general education designation. To ensure freshmen and sophomores could enroll in the course, EXPS 498/598—Exploring Writing with Children and Adolescents became EXPS 298—Writing to Communicate, Learn, and Teach. The revised course description states:

> This course provides a theoretical foundation for using writing to communicate and learn for personal and professional purposes. Emphasis will be placed on learning effective instructional strategies including modeling, using mentor text (high-quality writing examples to emulate), conferencing with others about one's writing, and peer and self-assessing of writing to support all writers' development. For the first half of the course, students will focus on developing their own writing skills using the writing process with three genres (narrative, informational/explanatory, and argument). Additional application of course knowledge will be demonstrated during the second half of the semester through academic service learning projects designed to teach elementary school students.

Using the same two ASL opportunities—writing clinic and YAF—the course continued with eight preservice teachers enrolled with two differences. Because the former school withdrew due to budget cuts, we collaborated with another local school; however, the principal canceled the writing clinic the day before it was scheduled to begin. A week later, with 24 registered students, we hosted the first two of ten sessions scheduled for the university writing clinic. For the tenth session, award-winning author, Diane Bradley, shared her revision process for her *Wilder's Trilogy*. Then the students shared their own nonfiction pieces. The writing clinic provided an authentic learning opportunity for everyone involved.

For the YAF, preservice teachers provided two 50-minute sessions (content repeated) and learned from Newbery winner, Christopher Paul Curtis. Mr. Curtis entertained the audience with his writing experiences and excerpt read alouds of his book, *The Watsons Go To Birmingham, 1967*.

Fourth Session

For Fall 2017 the course included 21 preservice teachers and became a requirement of the elementary educator preparation program. We provided a seven-session writing clinic during a local school's afterschool program. The K-5 urban elementary school served 400 students, of which 84% were White, 12.5% were African American, 3.0% were Latino/Hispanic, and 0.5% were Asian or American Indian or Alaskan Native. It is important to note this district is home to a large Arab/Arab-American population and many individuals report as White because the demographic category, Middle East and North Africa (MENA), which may be a choice families would check to represent their race and ethnicity, is not yet an option. As a Title I school, 84.5% received free/reduced lunch. This school was one of two elementary schools in a district that included 1 middle school and 2 high schools, serving 2,300 students overall.

For the writing clinic celebration, families filled the cafeteria. Many third-grade students read aloud their nonfiction writing to their families, peers, and preservice teachers from the stage. Certainly, not every writing clinic participant loved writing, but as the following post-course interview quote reveals, one third-grade student gained confidence to share his writing idea with the audience:

> A negative experience I've had was helping a certain child with his writing. He was so out of it and he didn't care much about it. He just slacked off nonstop. But me knowing that I'm going to be a future teacher, I knew I was not supposed to give up on him. So, I kept fighting through with him until he eventually became more comfortable with me and he was more comfortable in front of his peers. So, we talked about his writing piece in front of people and that was heartwarming because I was the reason why he did that, why he was finally comfortable.
> (Isla, Post-Course Interview, February 1, 2018)

For the 2017 YAF, preservice teachers led two 50-minute breakout sessions and listened to Matt Faulkner highlight his experiences as a children's book author and illustrator. He shared details about the book Kristen Remenar, his wife, wrote and he illustrated, *Groundhog's Dilemma*.

Fifth and Sixth Sessions

For Fall 2018 an additional course change related to the YAF was needed. Since 2013, when we first hosted the YAF, another course I teach, *Literature for Children*, requires preservice teachers to provide the breakout sessions. Because the YAF does not need two courses of preservice teachers to teach the instructional breakout sessions for third- through fifth-grade students, the preservice teachers enrolled in the writing methodology course provided poster presentations for families.

The week following the YAF, preservice teachers flipped the poster presentation content they presented to families in-person to instruct families using Google's Screencastify software. The YAF committee selected some of the flipped family resources to post to the YAF website's family resources page. The YAF created this webpage due to families requesting resources; thus, the flipped family resource is another ASL project. This new course requirement of creating a family resource, repeated for Fall 2019, helps ensure preservice teachers are empowered with the tools they may use as inservice teachers to flip their own writing workshop components to teach their future students to connect with families.

Also benefiting from the YAF as contest evaluators and audience participants, preservice teachers experience firsthand the influential effects of a published children's book author on students, families, and teachers. For 2018, preservice teachers observed the influence Mark Crilly, author/illustrator of the Akiko series, had on the awestruck students. Jean Alicia Elster, author of *The Colored Car*, shared her writing experiences for the 2019 YAF. The course requirements will continue through Fall 2020 when the YAF honoraria, author/illustrator, wife/husband team, Sarah and David Small share their experiences during the Fall 2020 YAF.

Transfer of Learning

The overall purpose for flipping the course is to ensure preservice teachers learn both writing content and pedagogy since teaching only content or only pedagogy does not prepare preservice teachers for all they will be tasked with as teachers of writing (Shulman, 1987). Such learning must transfer to their future classrooms. As inservice teachers, they will need to teach writing effectively as the following preservice teacher's comment illustrates:

> I really think that course you taught us was extremely valuable, and I would hope eventually that every preservice teacher will have to take that course, because I feel so much more confident leaving with all these strategies that I learned. I wouldn't feel this way going into my student teaching now had I not had that class. And I feel like, definitely, it's necessary because in reading methods you can only tackle writing so much, and I feel like an entire course devoted to it is exactly what we need because I feel that's an area that is neglected.
>
> (Harper, Post-Course Interview, February 12, 2015)

References

Abeysekera, L., & Dawson, P. (2015). Motivation and cognitive load in the flipped classroom: Definition, rationale and a call for research. *Higher Education Research & Development, 34*(1), 1–14. doi:10.1080/07294360.2014.934336

Atwell, N. (1998). *In the middle: New understandings about writing, reading, and learning.* Boynton/Cook Publishers, Inc.

Beckelhimer, L. (2015). Harnessing technology to help students reveal an authentic research process: Pictorial and video research steps. In A.G. Scheg (Ed.),

Implementation and critical assessment of the flipped classroom experience (pp. 246–273). Information Science Reference. doi:10.4018/978-1-4666-7464-6.ch013

Brenner, D., & McQuirk, A. (2019). A snapshot of writing in elementary teacher preparation programs. *The New Educator, 15*(1), 18–29. doi:10.1080/1547688X.2018.1427291

Bringle, R.G., & Hatcher, J.A. (1996). Implementing service learning in higher education. *Journal of Higher Education, 67*(2), 221–239.

Brooks, A.W. (2014). Information literacy and the flipped classroom: Examining the impact of a one-shot flipped class on student learning and perceptions. *Communications in Information Literacy, 8*(2), 225–235.

Buitrago, C.R., & Diaz J. (2016). *Our experience flipping EFL at Universidad de la Sabana in Colombia.* https://flippedlearning.org/grade_level/higher_ed/our-experience-flipping-efl-at-universidad-de-la-sabana-in-colombia/

Collier, S.M., Scheld, S., Barnard, I., & Stallcup, J. (2015). The negotiation and development of writing teacher identities in elementary education. *Teaching/Writing: The Journal of Writing Teacher Education, 4*(2), 90–112. http://scholarworks.wmich.edu/wte/vol4/iss2/6/

Cremin, T., & Myhill, D. (2012). *Writing voices: Creating communities of writers.* Routledge. doi:10.4324/9780203803332

Crisafulli, S. (2015). Flipping the composition classroom. In A.G. Scheg (Ed.), *Implementation and critical assessment of the flipped classroom experience* (pp. 41–59). Information Science Reference. doi:10.4018/978-1-4666-7464-6.ch003

DeFauw, D.L. (2017). Writing with parents in response to picture book read alouds. *Reading Horizons: A Journal of Literacy and Language Arts, 56*(2), 22–51. http://scholarworks.wmich.edu/reading_horizons/vol56/iss2/3/

DeFauw, D.L., Kriigel, B., & Samet, R. (2017). The University of Michigan – Dearborn's annual young authors' festival. *Michigan Reading Journal, 50*(1), 35–40.

DeFauw, D.L., & Smith, M. (2016). Writing for an authentic audience – One teacher-writer's narrative journey. *Teaching/Writing: The Journal of Writing Teacher Education, 5*(1), 104–126. http://scholarworks.wmich.edu/wte/vol5/iss1/7/

Englert, C.S., Mariage, T.V., & Dunsmore, K. (2006). Tenets of sociocultural theory in writing instruction research. In C.A. MacArthur, S. Graham, & J. Fitzgerald (Eds.), *Handbook of writing research* (pp. 208–221). The Guilford Press.

Flipped Learning Network. (2014). *What is flipped learning?* http://flippedlearning.org/wp-content/uploads/2016/07/FLIP_handout_FNL_Web.pdf

Flower, L., & Hayes, J.R. (1981). A cognitive process theory of writing. *College Composition and Communication, 32*(4), 365–387. doi:10.2307/356600

Flower, L., & Hayes, J.R. (1984). *Perspectives in writing research.* The Guildford Press.

Graves, D.H. (1983). *Writing: Teachers & children at work.* Heinemann.

Grimsley, C.R. (2015). How students in a first-year composition course respond to the flipped classroom. In A.G. Scheg (Volume Ed.), *Implementation and critical assessment of the flipped classroom experience* (pp. 99–118). Information Science Reference. doi:10.4018/978-1-4666-7464-6.ch006

Hart, S. (2007). Service-learning and literacy motivation: Setting a research agenda. In S.B. Gelmon & S.H. Billig (Eds.). *From passion to objectivity: International and cross- disciplinary perspectives on service-learning research* (pp. 135–156). Information Age Publishing, Inc.

Hawkins, L.K., Martin, N.M., & Cooper, J. (2019). Preparing elementary writing teachers: An inquiry-driven, field-based approach to instruction. *Teaching/Writing: The Journal of Writing Teacher Education, 6*(1), 132–160. https://scholarworks.wmich.edu/wte/vol6/iss1/8

Herrington, A., & Herrington, J. (2006). What is an authentic learning environment. In A. Herrington & J. Herrington (Eds.), *Authentic learning environments in higher education* (pp. 1–14). Information Science Publishing.

Hoffman, E.S. (2014). Beyond the flipped classroom: Redesigning a research methods course for e^3 instruction. *Contemporary Issues in Education Research, 7*(1), 51–62. doi:10.19030/cier.v7i1.8312

Howard, J.P.F. (1998). Academic service learning: A counternormative pedagogy. *New Direction for Teaching and Learning, 73*, 21–29. doi:10.1002/tl.7303

International Literacy Association (ILA) and National Council of Teachers of English (NCTE). (2017). *Literacy teacher preparation [Research advisory].* https://www.literacyworldwide.org/docs/default-source/where-we-stand/ila-ncte-teacher-prep-advisory.pdf

Kennedy, M.M. (1998). *Learning to teach writing: Does teacher education make a difference?* Teachers College Press.

Lave, J., & Wenger, E. (1991). *Situated learning: Legitimate peripheral participation.* Cambridge University Press. doi:10.1017/CBO9780511815355

Lenski, S., Ganske, K., Chambers, S., Wold, L., Dobler, E., Grisham, D.L., Scales, R., Smetana, L., Wolsey, T.D., Yoder, Y.Y., & Young, J. (2013). Literacy course priorities and signature aspects of nine elementary initial licensure programs. *Literacy Research and Instruction, 42*(1), 1–27. doi:10.1080/19388071.2012.738778

Locke, T. (2015). *Developing writing teachers: Practical ways for writers to transform their classroom practice.* Routledge. doi:10.4324/9780203096451

Martin, S.D., & Dismuke, S. (2015). Teacher candidates' perceptions of their learning and engagement in a writing methods course. *Teaching and Teacher Education, 46*, 104–114. doi:10.1016/j.tate.2014.11.002

Moffett, J. (2015). Twelve tips for "flipping" the classroom. *Medical Teacher, 37*(4), 331–336. doi:10.3109/0142159X.2014.943710

Morgan, D. (2010). Preservice teachers as writers. *Literacy Research and Instruction, 49*(4), 352–365. doi:10.1080/19388070903296411

Myers, J., Sanders, J., Ikpeze, C.H., Yoder, K.K., Scales, R.Q., Tracy, K.N., Smetana, L., & Grisham, D.L. (2019). Exploring connections between writing methods teacher education courses and K-12 field experience. *Action in Teacher Education, 41*(4), 344–360. doi:10.1080/01626620.2019.1600600

National Assessment of Education Progress (NAEP). (2019). *Writing.* https://nces.ed.gov/nationsreportcard/writing/

National Assessment of Education Progress (NAEP). (n.d.). *The nation's report card.* https://www.nationsreportcard.gov/

National Writing Project. (2020). *What we do.* https://www.nwp.org/what-we-do

Pajares, F., & Valiante, G. (2006). Self-efficacy beliefs and motivation in writing development. In C.A. MacArthur, S. Graham, & J. Fitzgerald (Eds.), *Handbook of writing research* (pp. 158–170). Guildford Press.

Prodoehl, D.E. (2015). Flipping first-year English: Strengthening teacher-student conferencing through online modules. In A.G. Scheg (Volume Ed.), *Implementation and critical assessment of the flipped classroom experience* (pp. 1–24). Information Science Reference. doi:10.4018/978-1-4666-7464-6.ch001

Rochester, S.E., Hwang, H.J., Wise, C.N., & Duke, N.K. (2018). Lessons learned: Applying the flipped classroom approach to a preservice teacher literacy methods course. *Literacy Practice & Research, 43*(3), 16–23.

Shulman, L.S. (1987). Knowledge and teaching: Foundations of the new reform. *Harvard Educational Review, 57*(1), 1–23. doi:10.17763/haer.57.1.j463w79r56455411

Spiker, A. (2015). Building a bridge through writing: How teachers can practice their own writing to benefit their students. *Literacy Today, 33*(2), 34–35.

Stockinger, P.C. (2007). Living in, learning from, looking back, breaking through in the English language arts methods course: A case study of two preservice teachers. *English Education, 39*(3), 201–225.

Webb, M., & Doman, E. (2016). Does the flipped classroom lead to increased gains on learning outcomes in ESL/EFL contexts?. *The CATESOL Journal, 28*(1), 39–67.

Wenger, E., McDermott, R., & Snyder, W.M. (2002). *Cultivating communities of practice: A guide to managing knowledge.* Harvard Business School Press.

Whyte, A., Lazarte, A., Thompson, I., Ellis, N., Muse, A., & Talbot, R. (2007). The National Writing Project, teachers' writing lives, and student achievement in writing. *Action in Teacher Education, 29*(2), 5–16. doi:10.1080/01626620.2007.10463444

Zhonggen, Y., & Guifang, W. (2016). Academic achievements and satisfaction of the clicker-aided flipped business English writing class. *Educational Technology & Society, 19*(2), 298–312.

Zimmerman, B.S., Morgan, D.N., & Kidder-Brown, M.K. (2014). The use of conceptual and pedagogical tools as mediators of preservice teachers' perceptions of self as writers and future teachers of writing. *Action in Teacher Education, 36*, 141–156. doi:10.1080/01626620.2014.898598

2 Flipped Writing Methodology Course

Somersaulting through the Process

Even though I often felt nervous about flipping the writing methodology course, experiencing dizzying somersaults as I tried to figure out all the pieces to the puzzle, the investment of time, patience, and learning benefited my students and me. I hope to make the process easier for you. Throughout the five action steps outlined in this chapter, I will connect to the national standards, detail the in-class and outside-of-class components, and suggest tools you may use to flip your own writing methodology course.

Step One: Determine the Content You Need to Teach

As a teacher preparation institution, we are required to meet the Council for the Accreditation of Educator Preparation (CAEP) (2019) standards, developed in 2013, which encompass the Interstate New Teacher Assessment and Support Consortium (InTASC) standards (Council of Chief State School Officers, 2011). Through this course, I address the 10 InTASC standards per preservice teachers' developmental readiness and the first two CAEP Standards: (1) Content and Pedagogical Knowledge, and (2) Clinical Partnerships and Practices. Through the course, preservice teachers learn pedagogical content knowledge of writing (PCKW) they apply through academic service learning (ASL) opportunities.

All teacher educators of writing are tasked to meet the International Literacy Association (ILA) and National Council of Teachers of English's (NCTE) (2017) standards as we prepare literacy professionals to "develop and implement writing instruction that builds learners' understanding and use of the writing process and their ability to create original compositions of all genres" (p. 12). The following standards especially apply in elementary teacher preparation:

- Pre-K/Primary and Elementary/Intermediate Classroom teachers, per Standard 2.3, must be taught to "design, adapt, implement, and evaluate

evidence-based instruction and materials to develop writing processes and orthographic knowledge" (p. 79) that is developmentally appropriate for each learner; and
- Elementary/Intermediate Classroom teachers, per Standard 1.2, must "demonstrate knowledge of major theoretical, conceptual, and evidence-based foundations of elementary/intermediate writing development and the writing process and evidence-based instructional approaches that support writing of specific types of text and producing writing appropriate to task" (p. 77).

Per University requirements, I meet general education objectives, program learning goals, and course-specific goals. First, the Written and Oral Communication goals for the University of Michigan–Dearborn's Discovery Core (n.d.) are as follows:

1. "Students are able to compose, revise, and edit their own writing for clarity and fluency of expression.
2. Students are able to demonstrate how to prepare and adapt written and oral communication to the needs of multiple audiences across professional, academic, and interpersonal contexts.
3. Students are able to demonstrate an understanding of academic integrity and use research skills including evaluating information, writing from sources, and correctly citing works.
4. Students are able to critically evaluate and use readings and ideas in composing written or oral work" (n.p.).

Second, program learning goals specify candidates for certification will be (a) capable users of pedagogical knowledge, (b) reflective about their practice, and (c) capable in their content specialty areas. Third, course-specific goals require students to:

- Use the recursive writing process—prewriting, composing, revising, editing, and publishing—to express oneself clearly and fluently.
- Develop a teacher-writer identity that aligns with the National Writing Project's principles.
- Demonstrate how to prepare and adapt written and oral communication to the needs of multiple audiences across professional, academic, and interpersonal contexts.
- Demonstrate an understanding of academic integrity and use research skills including evaluating information, writing from sources, and correctly citing works.
- Critically evaluate readings and ideas used in composing written or oral work.

- Apply effective writing strategies and encourage students' writing through two ASL projects (Writing Clinic and Young Authors' Festival).
- Reflect on personal, academic, and social development as it relates to the ASL projects.

To encapsulate these learning objectives, the course description states the following:

> This course provides a theoretical foundation for using writing to communicate and learn for personal and professional purposes. Emphasis will be placed on learning effective instructional strategies including modeling, using mentor texts (high-quality writing examples to emulate), conferencing with others about one's writing, and peer-and self-assessing writing to support all writers' development. For the first half of the course, students will focus on developing their own writing skills using the writing process with three genres (narrative, informational/explanatory, and argument). Additional application of course knowledge will be demonstrated during the second half of the semester through two academic service learning projects designed to tutor young writers and support their families.

To prepare preservice teachers to teach K-12 writing standards, I address the Common Core State Standards (CCSS) (National Governors Association Center for Best Practices & Council of Chief State School Officers, 2010) throughout the course. Although I value all forms of writing, I focus on argument, informational/explanatory, and narrative genres per the CCSS. Additionally, preservice teachers read the English Language Arts CCSS: writing, reading, language, speaking, and listening. They (a) explore the anchor standards K-12 students need to meet to be college and career ready, and (b) utilize their students' grade-level CCSS for lesson development.

Needless to say, as teacher educators, we have ample PCKW to teach. I must teach the content within a semester-long course and flipped learning allows me to orchestrate opportunities to ensure preservice teachers learn efficiently. My ultimate goal with flipped learning is to ensure transfer of learning for preservice teachers from course content to field experiences to their future teaching contexts.

Step Two: Choose to Use Flipped Writing Pedagogies

Although there are myriad choices we make as teacher educators regarding how we deliver required content, I argue an important choice is to use flipped learning to use time efficiently. Dickenson (2014) compared a flipped and a traditional version of a monthly student teaching seminar. Teacher self-efficacy was significantly stronger for student teachers enrolled in the flipped course as more in-person class time provided opportunities for mastery learning through peer collaboration, presentation of content, instructor/peer feedback, and practice teaching.

To provide preservice teachers opportunities to practice teaching, Rochester et al. (2018) flipped a K-2 literacy methods course taught in an elementary school. Outside of class, preservice teachers learned content through such tools as pre-recorded lectures and videos. They completed reflective writing and required readings, designed lesson plans and assessments, and wrote case study reports of their target students in their co-requisite field experiences. To support mastery learning, in-class time was devoted to guided practice as preservice teachers observed the professor's and other inservice teachers' English language arts instruction and assessment with the elementary students. The flipped learning design ensured preservice teachers practiced content learned outside of class before they engaged with students in the field experience. Evidence demonstrated preservice teachers learned the content and enjoyed the flipped learning structure.

I choose flipped learning to support preservice teachers' transfer of PCKW to authentic learning contexts. Preservice teachers use our learning management system, Canvas, outside of class, to participate in pre-recorded lectures, read assigned texts, and discuss course content. In-person, preservice teachers engage in authentic literacy tasks, professional learning communities, and teaching contexts. In-person time is used to participate in writing workshop where preservice teachers make writerly choices as we explore each session's genre-specific topic. (See Appendix for session topics.) The in-person class sessions include a 10-minute mini lesson used to begin each session's forty-five-minute writing workshop and thirty-minute professional learning tasks completed at the end of each in-person session.

Across all course sessions (Tuesdays and Thursdays, 3:30 pm–4:45 pm) during each Fall semester, preservice teachers participate in writing workshop for 32% of the sessions and professional learning communities (PLCs) for 22% of the sessions. The PLCs are designed for collaborative planning for ASL projects aside from three in-person sessions focused on evaluating writing contests. My hope was that identifying the small group collaboration as a PLC would create a student-centered habit of mind preservice teachers would bring to the group work (Vescio et al., 2008).

During the second half of the semester, preservice teachers participate in two ASL projects—writing clinic and Young Authors' Festival (YAF)—which encompass 46% of the sessions. The writing clinic is designed to support local elementary students' writing development. Students and sometimes their families meet with us at the elementary school during our usual face-to-face timeframe to participate in the writing clinic. The YAF project, a collaborative opportunity co-developed with the librarians at the Mardigian Library and other community members, is designed to celebrate literacy with elementary students and their families. Through both ASL projects, preservice teachers reflect on students' writing development as they interact with one to three elementary students through the writing clinic, evaluate the writing contest entries third- through fifth-grade students submit for the YAF writing contest, and interact with the families at the YAF.

Using flipped learning is a choice, a choice my students support as evident in the anonymous course evaluations detailed in Table 2.1 and 24 comments. The lowest score occurred due to the last-minute writing clinic's cancellation at a local school for Fall 2016. We scrambled to reschedule a University-hosted, ten-session writing clinic that also proved too demanding for a 200-level course. For example, in my field note journal, I detailed the following observation:

> I walked into the classroom a bit early to find 4 of my 8 students talking about the course. I could tell from the tones the conversation was not positive; thus, I opened discussion right away. Annie (a senior) shared the course feels too demanding. She is uncomfortable that I have added two additional assignments and she has to provide weekly lesson plans to submit for ten writing clinic sessions. She is also concerned that they cannot meet with me. Students did not understand that with the change from [the local school] to the on-campus writing clinic, that our time to meet together would not occur (due to transportation for families). To support students, I let them know the two assignments I added are a way for me to double check their progress with their argument writing piece, to run electronic writing conferences. I learned that I also included too many writing-clinic sessions. I'll provide them lesson plans for each session they may choose to use, or they can create their own.

With ASL courses, I have learned to invite students' concerns so I may make changes to ease students' workloads whenever possible. Nine comments preservice teachers offered through the course evaluations highlight recommendations for improving the course's pacing, especially reducing the number of writing-clinic sessions as the following comments illustrate:

- I would either spend a few class sessions preparing for the writer's clinic, or have the writer's clinic once a week for 5 (or even more) weeks so that we had the weekend to prepare for the next session.
- I wonder if in future semesters, the writing clinic starts on a Thursday, which gives the class a chance to focus on expectations, preparation,

Table 2.1 Course Evaluations: Overall Assessment of the Course

Semester	Return Rate	Excellent (5)	Above Average (4)	Average (3)	Below Average (2)	Poor (1)	Mean
F '14	25/26	24	0	1	0	0	4.92
F '16	8/8	3	4	0	1	0	4.13
F '17	19/21	16	2	1	0	0	4.79
F '18	22/25	17	4	1	0	0	4.73
F '19	15/20	14	1	0	0	0	4.93

and have the opportunity to ask questions on a Tuesday. It would also give students the weekend to reflect on that first session, prepare for future sessions, as well as have plenty of time to figure out and resolve any issues that have arisen by discussing them with peers in the online discussion board.

Five out of 24 comments address flipped learning components or the writing clinic's start, at which point our in-person sessions evolve from writing workshop and PLC sessions into small-group or one-on-one tutoring sessions:

- The online Voicethreads were an asset. The modules supported my understanding of what it means to be a teacher-writer and gave me knowledge of strategies to become a more effective teacher-writer.
- The pace picked up drastically toward the end of the semester in terms of assignments being due around the Thanksgiving period where our main focus shifts to the writing clinic, which can be a bit difficult. However, with proper balance, everything can be achieved successfully.
- Inspired me to write more and eventually be a published writer. I thought there were too many assignments at times and it was hard to take a breather which required students to be extra organized as many assignments overlapped at times.

The overlap of assignments related to the two field experience journal entries preservice teachers submit weekly for feedback. Additionally, their writer's notebooks are due with their formative assessments for half of the modules and some preservice teachers manage their time better than others. Module completion is graded weekly, but some preservice teachers use their notes to complete their formative assessments after the modules' weekly due dates.

Twelve comments focus on the ASL opportunities the flipped learning course design made possible, which the following comments illustrate:

- I also loved how I had the chance to work with students on two different occasions—The Author's Festival and Writing Clinic. ... It raised my confidence in teaching writing to students.
- Love that we were able to do the writing clinic, as well as the Young Authors' Festival. I learned a plethora of strategies of how to incorporate writing in my future classroom.

Analyzing interview data, I found it interesting that preservice teachers did not mention the flipped learning pedagogy unless I asked about the flipped writing methodology course design purposefully. Even when

I prompted, "Discuss your experience with flipped learning," participants often asked me to clarify unless they completed the flipped learning family resource, a course requirement as of Fall 2018. Aside from one course evaluation comment—"I felt as though I would have learned more if the course was more classroom based where we would learn in class as opposed to online"—the data show that for the participants, the content was not perceived any differently than if we had discussed the topics in class. When I asked the preservice teachers about the flipped writing methodology course design, they mentioned the modules, as the following comments illustrate:

- I thought the flipped classroom with the modules online was really helpful because that was a lot of stuff that you could do on your own and to do that in class would have just kind of been … odd because we all would've been sitting silently and not really helping each other out.

  (Post-Course Interview, February 19, 2019)

- I enjoyed it because we're able to focus on our writing in class, but learn more in depth about certain topics at home. The hard part, I guess, would be saying, like disciplining myself to stay on track with it, to make sure that I'm doing the PowerPoints and not waiting until the last minute to listen to the lecture before it's due.

  (Post-Course Interview, January 22, 2020)

For me, flipping the course content felt like an extreme measure, but students did not see the course design in the same way. They simply completed the modules and learned, which I think shows the students' comfort level with technology. Preservice teachers adapted, quicker than myself, with changes in course delivery.

Step Three: Select Content to Deliver through Flipped Writing Pedagogies

When I contemplate the number of puzzle pieces I have to fit together to teach PCKW, I identify key content, guided by the literature and standards (e.g., Graham et al., 2015; Graham & Perin, 2007; ILA & NCTE, 2017), preservice teachers need to understand in order to develop their PCKW. Ultimately, I aim to prepare preservice teachers for teaching within the writing clinic and their future contexts as student and inservice teachers.

I align modules with content they need to learn independently before they apply what they have learned in-person. For example, Module 1 addresses two topics: teacher-writers and writing workshop, which we begin to address in-person during the first week of class. Preservice teachers have a week to complete the following Module 1 components:

- Listen to teacher-writers Voicethread lecture.
- View teacher-writers lecture PowerPoint.
- View two author interviews addressing freewriting.
- Review my authority list.
- Read my short piece: DeFauw, D.L. (2010). A challenge to write. *The Reading Teacher*, 64(5), 374, 10.1598/RT.64.5.11.
- Listen to writing workshop framework Voicethread lecture.
- View writing workshop framework lecture PowerPoint.
- Review mini lessons.
- Complete Module 1's try-it tasks in writer's notebook.

Additional modules include each component of the writing process, especially conferencing and revising. A week prior to each ASL opportunity, preservice teachers complete modules on (a) writing assessment to support the contest evaluation process, (b) YAF, and (c) writing clinic. Additionally, because we do not participate in writing workshop during the second half of the semester, students explore modules on the narrative and argument genres.

The Appendix details the modules' topics and required try-it tasks I include as formative assessments to monitor preservice teachers' module completion. I noted in a Fall 2016 memo my concern that some preservice teachers had not listened to the online lectures; thus, I needed to monitor module completion through Canvas' course analytics and prerequisite module requirements. For example, students cannot open Module 2 until they have completed Module 1. I also require they take notes as they engage with the modules. Since Fall 2016, I grade for module completion because if the modules do not receive a grade, students may not perceive the flipped learning components as time-worthy (de Oliveira Fassbinder et al., 2014). Preservice teachers demonstrate module completion per Canvas analytics and detailed notes with completed try-it tasks in their writer's notebooks.

Step Four: Determine the Resources You Have Available to Flip Course Content

To flip a lecture, you need to create a screencast, which is a video recording of your computer screen with your voice lecturing content. Use familiar tools with screencasting software, such as PowerPoint, Google slides, or Microsoft Word. For me, I use PowerPoint or Google slides to highlight my key points concerning PCKW. I use the screencasting software to record my lecture as I flip through the slides, lecturing as I would in-person. The only downside is I cannot read my audience's body language so I have to anticipate which details need more or less explanation. Cockrum (2014) recommends teachers write their lectures and then read them.

In addition to the lectures, sometimes I read aloud a short excerpt from a mentor text, always adhering to copyright laws. Also, I open Microsoft Word documents and model writing, which is recorded with the screencasting software. Johansen and Cherry-Paul (2016) have used video recording equipment to capture their writing in their writer's notebooks. Whatever teachers would do for an in-person mini lesson or a lecture, they can do through a flipped lesson using screencasting software; thus, any mini lesson can be flipped. For example, as highlighted on my website (danielledefauw.com), I teach students to notice and name effective word choice while reading April Pulley Sayre's, *Turtle, Turtle, Watch Out!*. I could just as easily create PowerPoint slides highlighting the key points and use screencasting software to lecture and model how I notice what Sayre does with her word choice. I could also model how I choose to write like Sayre using the same screencasting software to capture my writing in a Word document.

As a teacher educator, I still choose to teach a mini lesson at the start of each writing workshop session. You certainly could require students to listen to mini lessons outside of class as Cockrum (2014) does, but as a teacher educator, I need to model how to run a complete writing workshop. The data supports this as participants state they need more experience with managing the writing workshop, as Roberta shared in her post-course interview on February 9, 2017: "I have confidence in myself that I can work well and effectively in a small group setting with student writers, but I have yet to see how that looks in a large group."

To support preservice teachers, much of the online content I provide is focused not on mini-lesson content, but on writer's craft and pedagogy. With just the right tools in my hand, I can teach more content in less time and save in-person time for demonstrating the PCKW I want preservice teachers to transfer to their future teaching contexts.

Step Five: Flip Course Content to Facilitate Flipped Learning

To flip course content, I use the screencasting software, Kaltura, which I have access to through the University's learning management system, Canvas. When I first started with screencasting, I used Voicethread, so I pay a yearly membership. My Voicethread lectures are available on my website, danielledefauw.com. I do not consider my screencasts model examples. Like me, Garver (2016) flipped a course using PowerPoint and 30- to 45-minute lectures, but he states those screencasts were a "big mistake" as he now creates shorter podcasts using "music, pictures, and videos to achieve maximum impact" (p. 95). I continue to learn how to improve delivery of online content, and in due time, I plan to make my lectures more engaging.

If you do not have access to a learning management system, you may consider using Google Suite. To use Google Suite, you need a Google account, which can be created at www.google.com with any email address. If you do have a gmail address, you already have access to the Google Suite, which includes Google docs, slides, forms, drive, etc. The drive is invaluable for storing your flipped learning materials. Better yet, creating a Google classroom would allow you to create your own type of learning management system for your preservice teachers. The screencasting software available through Google Suite is Screencastify, which is an add-on for the Chrome browser, if you are a Chrome user. You can also download Screencastify from your app store. The free version has a five-minute time limit. It used to have a ten-minute time limit which I used to ensure concise lectures.

There are many screencasting software options that a quick Google search will reveal. You may consider using Camtasia (https://techsmith.com/video-editor.html), Screencast-o-Matic (https://screencast-o-matic.com/), or OBS Studio (https://obsproject.com/). Use any screencasting tool to record your voice and actions on your electronic device as you lead your students through mini lessons or lectures. Creating screencasts is time consuming; however, once they are created they can be reused in various contexts.

Remember, flipping content does not mean preservice teachers will engage in flipped learning (Talbert, 2017). As teacher educators, we must thread connections between outside-of-class instruction and in-person application to ensure flipped learning is achieved. Preservice teachers need to *own* the choice to build their foundational understanding through flipped content that must be instrumental to their active engagement with content in-person to develop the PCKW they need to learn, understand, apply, and transfer.

References

Cockrum, T. (2014). *Flipping your English class to reach all learners: Strategies and lesson plans*. Routledge.

Council for the Accreditation of Educator Preparation (CAEP). (2019). *2013 CAEP standards*. http://caepnet.org/~/media/Files/caep/standards/caep-standards-one-pager-0219.pdf

Council of Chief State School Officers. (2011). *Interstate Teacher Assessment and Support Consortium (InTASC) model core teaching standards: A resource for state dialogue*. https://ccsso.org/sites/default/files/201711/InTASC_Model_Core_Teaching_Standards_2011.pdf

de Oliveira Fassbinder, A.G., Moreira, D., Cruz, G., & Barbosa, E.F. (2014). *Tools for the flipped classroom model: An experiment in teacher education*. IEEE.

Dickenson, P. (2014). Flipping the classroom in a teacher education course. In J. Keengwe, G. Onchwari, & J. Oigara (Eds.), *Promoting active learning through the flipped classroom model* (pp. 145–162). [Advances in Educational Technologies and Instructional Design (AETID) Book Series]. Information Science Reference. doi:10.4018/978-1-4666-4987-3.ch008

Garver, M.S. (2016). Flip don't flop: Best practices for flipping marketing courses. In J.B. Waldrop & M.A. Bowdon (Eds.), *Best practices for flipping the college classroom* (pp. 87–100). Routledge.

Graham, S., & Perin, D. (2007),. *Writing next: Effective strategies to improve writing of adolescents in middle and high schools*. Alliance for Excellent Education.

Graham, S., Harris, K.R., & Santangelo, T. (2015). Research-based writing practices and the common core: Meta-analysis and meta-synthesis. *The Elementary School Journal, 115*(4), 498–522. doi:10.1086/681964

International Literacy Association (ILA) and National Council of Teachers of English (NCTE). (2017). *Literacy teacher preparation [Research advisory]*. https://www.literacyworldwide.org/docs/default-source/where-we-stand/ila-ncte-teacher-prep-advisory.pdf

Johansen, D., & Cherry-Paul, S. (2016). *Flip your writing workshop: A blended learning approach*. Heinemann.

National Governors Association Center for Best Practices & Council of Chief State School Officers. (2010). *Common core state standards for English language arts and literacy in history/social studies, science, and technical subjects.* Authors. http://www.corestandards.org/ELA-Literacy/

Rochester, S.E., Hwang, H.J., Wise, C.N., & Duke, N.K. (2018). Lessons learned: Applying the flipped classroom approach to a preservice teacher literacy methods course. *Literacy Practice and Research, 43*(3), 16–23.

Talbert, R. (2017). *Flipped learning: A guide for higher education faculty*. Stylus Publishing.

University of Michigan – Dearborn. (n.d.). *Dearborn discovery core (general education)*. https://umdearborn.edu/faculty-staff/academic-program-and-course-development/dearborn-discovery-core-general-education

Vescio, V., Ross, D., & Adams, A. (2008). A review of research on the impact of professional learning communities on teaching practice and student learning. *Teaching and Teacher Education, 24*(1), 80–91. doi:10.1016/j.tate.2007.01.004

3 Writing Workshop

Writing for One Person to Make the Impossible Possible

When the flipped writing methodology course begins, preservice teachers participate in writing workshop, a framework for delivering writing process instruction, as they write informational/explanatory pieces for their future students. Preservice teachers use picture books as mentor texts, or texts they wish to emulate in their own writing (Cramer & Cramer, 1975). Like the young character in Sally Lloyd-Jones' (2019) *Look! I Wrote a Book! (And You Can Too!)*, illustrated by Neal Layton, preservice teachers experience the writing process from idea generation to publishing. This writing experience and others explored throughout the course allow preservice teachers to make writerly choices, choices that become threaded promises to encourage their future students' choices in writing topics, purposes, and audiences.

In this chapter, we will explore how the recursive writing process applies to the writing workshop framework, provided through the flipped writing methodology course, and how preservice teachers perceive the writing process. Next, we will discover the role audience plays in motivating preservice teachers' writing. Finally, we will address the first research question:

- Through a flipped writing methodology course, how will preservice teachers develop their teacher-writer identity and writing abilities through writing workshop?

Writing Workshop Framework

Preservice teachers develop stamina as they experience consistent instruction through writing workshop—mini lessons, independent writing, conferencing, and sharing—where they learn to solve their writing challenges through the writing process to support not only their own writing development, but also their future elementary students' writing development (Araujo et al., 2014). Through writing workshop instruction, teachers use a balanced approach focused on explicit writing skills and writing process strategies

(Cutler & Graham, 2008) that support students' metacognitive development (Englert et al., 1988).

I believe the writing workshop framework provides the most authentic means for writing instruction as writers participate in a community of practice (Lave & Wenger, 1991). As a writing workshop community, the writers learn together through shared experience (Wenger et al., 2002). Necessarily, students write through an authentic recursive writing process—prewriting/rehearsal, drafting, revising, editing, publishing/presenting—published authors use within a social atmosphere conducive to the writerly life (Graham et al., 2015). The flipped writing methodology course design facilitates preservice teachers' eight-week writing workshop participation. Throughout the writing process, like all effective writers, preservice teachers "have a concrete sense of their audience" (Barnard, 2014, p. 121) as they write the three genres the Common Core State Standards (CCSS) require K-12 students to write:

1. Preservice teachers write an informational/explanatory piece for their future elementary students during the first month of class for a chosen grade level and subject—social studies, science, math, etc.
2. Preservice teachers write an argument piece during the second and third month of class on a self-selected topic. They identify an authentic publication opportunity and may choose to submit their final copy for publication.
3. Preservice teachers write a personal narrative during the third and fourth month outside of class using Phillips and Larson's (2015) "Becoming Writer" prompts and flipped resources provided through our Canvas site. Their audience is someone special to whom they plan to gift their narrative.

For each required writing, I demonstrate my teacher-writer abilities (Kaufman, 2009). Although I consider myself a lifelong learner who will never achieve expertise, I believe preservice teachers need to observe my modeling of writing, which increases the course's authenticity (Atwell, 1998; Herrington et al., 2014). "In order to promote reflection, authentic and meaningful activities can be provided, together with access to expert performance and opinion to enable students to compare themselves to experts" (Herrington & Herrington, 2006, p. 7).

I model writing workshop components and expect preservice teachers to teach students similarly (Colby & Stapleton, 2006). The writing workshop framework provides preservice teachers with a structure to support elementary students' exploration of their writing processes; elementary students (a) learn writer's craft through mini lessons; (b) work in small groups of three to six students, teacher-led or peer-collaborative, to improve writing; (c) choose their own writing topics, purposes, and audiences; and (d) receive feedback from writing community members (Atwell, 1998).

Mini Lessons

To model the use of the writing workshop framework for preservice teachers, during the first half of each in-person session I teach a 10- to 15-minute mini lesson to model writing and teach students how to use mentor texts (Calkins, 2006). Stolarek (1994) used the term prose modeling: "the act of determining the defining characteristics of a model text, that is, a text which is seen as being exemplary of its kind, and developing methods of duplicating these defining characteristics using different content" (p. 154). Mentor texts include any published articles, my writing, a student's writing sample, or picture books (Dorfman & Cappelli, 2009). The CCSS recommend the use of mentor texts (Shanahan, 2015).

Research supports the use of mentor texts with upper elementary to secondary students (e.g., Graham & Perin, 2007; Premont et al., 2017; Pytash et al., 2014) and college students (Stolarek, 1994). Graham and Perin (2007) determined five out of six writing studies had a small yet positive effect size for studying mentor texts to support writing development. Stolarek (1994) divided 143 college freshmen and 21 published composition professors into five groups: (a) description; (b) model, or mentor text; (c) description and model; (d) model with explication; or (e) all instructional methods. Participants in the all-instructional-methods group performed best, supported through explicit explanation of genre models and characteristics. When using mentor texts, freshmen wrote more like professional writers.

Using mentor texts allows preservice teachers to develop their own writing and co-teach their future students with published authors. For example, preservice teachers can learn to pass time quickly in their narratives, emulating: (a) Rylant's (1985) *The Relatives Came* where she uses a single statement to encompass a day's travel; or (b) Woodson's (2004) *Coming On Home Soon* where she uses a two-word sentence to propel the reader into the future. For their informational/explanatory pieces, preservice teachers can learn to use the power of one as they follow a turtle's or spadefoot toad's life cycle in April Pulley Sayre's picture books: (a) *Turtle, Turtle, Watch Out!* (Sayre, 2010); and (b) *Dig, Wait, Listen: A Desert Toad's Tale* (Sayre, 2001). Following the storyline, Sayre provides ancillary material about "Sea Turtle Species" and "The Spadefoot Toad" written with an expository voice; thus, each book includes two mentor texts for each topic. For their argument pieces, I offer preservice teachers the article Melissa Smith and I wrote following the course's first semester (DeFauw & Smith, 2016). We also study Newsela.com articles, *New York Times* articles, and picture books recommended by Getz's

(2018) blogpost *Mentor Texts for Teaching Argument Writing*. Preservice teachers need to practice using mentor texts to support their revision processes as they use writer's craft like the authors they read.

Revision Mini Lessons

Of all the layers to the writing process, modeling revision strategies is imperative. I model revision of my own genre pieces to demonstrate the revision strategies preservice teachers must learn to use as writers and teach to their students. Dorn and Soffos (2001) stated, "Revision relates to the meaning level ... [and] can occur along a continuum of easier to harder tasks" (p. 6). To achieve these tasks, preservice teachers use revision-focused vocabulary in mini lessons (Hooper et al., 2006) to teach strategies such as adding details, organizing text, using specific word choice, crafting varied sentences, and reading text aloud. All writers need to practice rereading and re-seeing their writing (Graves, 2004), which require explicit revision strategies such as adding extra paragraphs to add details, reordering details, and showing versus telling content (Calkins, 2006). Writers reread their pieces to ensure their writer's voice reflects their intended messages (Graves, 2004). Even a writer, let alone a reader, can get lost in the details without an organized structure (Portalupi & Fletcher, 2004). Revision requires practice, but preservice teachers and their future elementary students need to see revision strategies modeled through mini lessons so they understand how to revise.

The choice to view revision as an invitation versus a punishment for not writing well is an important step in any writer's development (Heard, 2002). Harper noted in her field note journal a revision focus in the parent session she attended in Fall 2014:

> I can tell the families are really opening up and enjoying the writing clinic ... One of my favorite aspects of this session was how we used literature to name how authors write, and attempted to write like them as we revised our pieces. This session inspired me to reflect on how I feel about revision, how I have used revision in the past, and how I can teach revision to my future students and in future practice. I, much like many children, think the task of revision is daunting. I often forget that your first draft doesn't have to be pretty. We can add dialogue, draw lines, scribble out, so on and so forth. I always focus too much on attempting to make my first draft as perfect as it can possibly be in the hopes that I have minimal revisions to do. However, I know that this is not best practice and the most effective strategy. When working with students, it will be great to model for them the revision process, and I just need to keep in mind that REVISION IS OKAY! It is an essential part of the

writing process, and though it may seem daunting, it helps make our writing stronger. Having a positive attitude about revision will show my students that it is okay, and can even be fun, and this family session showed me a few strategies for inspiring revision (five senses, dialogue) that I will be able to use in my future practice.

Through course content, we focus on revision as I think it is the most important yet least understood component of the writing process. I require preservice teachers to revise all three genre pieces throughout the semester to experience revision's power to transform writing.

Using Google docs, I require preservice teachers to revise their drafts based on their peers' and my feedback using Google's suggesting feature before final-grade submission. Preservice teachers must practice revision if they will ever teach revision well. I model providing formative feedback using Google's suggesting and comment features so that preservice teachers revise their writing based on formative feedback. Preservice teachers need to anticipate the development their own students will demonstrate when formative feedback is used to support their writing development (Graham et al., 2015).

Initially, preservice teachers often focus on editing versus revision when providing feedback, even though preservice teachers have experienced the "red-pen" effects. Serene stated in her writing history essay, "I hated getting back essays and papers with red ink all over! This really made me lose confidence in my writing. As a future teacher I do not want to own a red ink pen (maybe purple)!" Focused on revision strategies, our writing workshop community practices using writer's craft language, especially while conferencing, to help all writers control the complex communication processes writing entails and revision supports (Lane, 1993).

Independent Writing and Conferencing

Following each mini lesson, preservice teachers write for 30 minutes per the in-person genre focus (informational/explanatory or argument). I encourage preservice teachers to write their first draft in their writer's notebooks, a composition notebook, before moving onto their electronic devices to use Google docs. Although most preservice teachers prefer typing, the focus on handwriting in their writer's notebooks is twofold. First, I want preservice teachers to fill a writer's notebook with their writing to show their future students. Their students will see them as teacher-writers and feel motivated, likely, to fill their own writer's notebooks (DeFauw, 2016). Second, I want preservice teachers to experience handwriting difficulties. Preservice teachers often complain about their hands hurting due to the physical strain handwriting requires. I remind preservice teachers their future students will also have to develop their handwriting stamina during independent writing time. Whether preservice teachers use handwriting or typing, I ask them to try the mini lesson task presented before choosing another writing focus for their draft during the independent writing time.

As preservice teachers make writerly choices, I have discovered independent writing time usually is community focused. Although I am a teacher-writer who prefers silence during independent writing, I have learned many preservice teachers need vibrant social interaction to support their writing processes.

Hillocks (1984) described writing instruction's social element as the environmental mode of instruction. Writing workshop's social dynamics ensure all classroom resources, especially the expertise and learning processes of students, are used fully to help the writing community thrive; thus, I encourage preservice teachers to peer conference, a task we model early in the semester. I also conduct one-on-one or small-group conferences, which I consider the central component of a writing workshop. While conferencing, I am transparent about how I set up conferences, why I suggest certain teaching points, and when I am struggling to identify a teaching point. Preservice teachers need to understand all teachers experience challenges with writing instruction.

Purposefully, I catch and release our writing community (Bennett, 2007). For example, during a writing conference, I might catch the class's attention to highlight character action in a preservice teacher's writing. I demonstrate for preservice teachers Bennett's (2007) catch and release technique and note the technique's benefits in teaching during independent writing time to provide a teaching point, highlight a writer's skill, and release the writing community back to independent writing so everyone creates content to share.

Sharing

Writers need to share their writing with an authentic audience throughout their writing processes. As preservice teachers write, they understand their audience includes themselves and present or future readers (Ede & Lunsford, 1984), such as their peers, students, and professional stakeholders. They share for five minutes with partners, small groups, or whole group following a writing workshop session. To be honest, due to scarcity of time, I rush through sharing too often even though I know sharing allows writers to witness an audience's reactions, questions, comments, and concerns. Such feedback is welcomed from a writing community's audience facilitated through authentic literacy activities:

> [Authentic literacy activities] replicate or reflect reading and writing activities that occur in the lives of people outside of a

learning-to-read-and-write context and purpose. Each authentic literacy activity has a writer and a reader – a writer who is writing to a real reader and a reader who is reading what the writer wrote.

(Duke et al., 2006, p. 346)

Without audience, writing is inauthentic; granted, the audience could be the writer, but even writing for oneself requires preservice teachers to face writing challenges as Jowan shared:

> That's the hardest part for me: it's to actually sit down and actually write ... Sometimes I feel like the hardest part is when I'm writing just journal entries for myself and I'm writing just ... personal things I feel like I don't want to write it ... I don't want someone to see it so ... I don't write as much as I should.
>
> (Jowan Nabha, Post-Course Interview, February 9, 2018)

As writers choose their audience, the desire to share their writing with actual readers who want to read their inherent messages strengthens (Conference on College Composition and Communication, 1989/2013/2015). Lindblom (2015) stated, "When a writer makes his or her own decisions about the writing, that gives the writer real authority. That word itself shows how important this is: author-ity" (n.p.). The more responsive the audience, the more writers care to influence their audience with their messages (Wiggins, 2009). I challenge preservice teachers to write as teacher-writers across genres for myriad purposes and authentic audiences so they are prepared to support their future students' transfer of learning through authentic writing instruction.

Developing Teacher-Writer Identities through Writing Workshop

The flipped writing methodology course design creates space for preservice teachers' writing workshop participation (Bergmann et al., 2015). The writing assignments propel preservice teachers to propose a reason for the writing, communicate with a real audience, and use genre features to receive real reactions from an audience (Lindblom, 2004). Preservice teachers experience the challenges and benefits of writing for specific audiences as they create a community of writers, reading and writing various genres, improving their writer's craft through the writing process, and presenting their writing. Developing their understanding as teacher-writers through authentic literacy activities improves their abilities to teach writing as preservice and inservice teachers.

Regarding the first research question driving this study—Through a flipped writing methodology course, how will preservice teachers develop their teacher-writer identity and writing abilities through writing workshop?—the data demonstrate that although preservice teachers develop their writing abilities through writing workshop, preservice teachers do not self-identify as teacher-writers during the course. The data reveal only Roberta, a published children's book author, self-identified as a teacher-writer during the course. Interestingly, the data show an active process of identifying as a teacher-writer, meaning the process evolves throughout the participants' writerly experiences (Elf, 2017; Ivanič, 2006). Participants select audiences for their writing pieces, during and after the course, which demonstrate this process of identification as the following three examples illustrate.

First, Maceo asked me if I knew how to access our longstanding University of Michigan–Dearborn's publication, *The Michigan Journal*. I asked if he planned to publish in the journal. He smiled and said, "I want to surprise you." On October 22, 2019, Maceo sent me two separate emails:

> I just want to thank you for opening my eyes to the world of writing and really helping me find a joy for it. I would've never had this article published if it wasn't for you giving us all of those sources in the modules. I really appreciate your class and the opportunity you've opened for me. The exciting news is that if I write one more article, I'll be an official staff editor for *The Michigan Journal*!

> Just got some more super exciting news. I will be writing an article to promote the Young Authors' Festival that is planned to be published under the student life section of *The Michigan Journal*.

Maceo's data does not mention a teacher-writer identity although he did self-identify as a writer; however, seeking publication, modeling writing for his students during the writing clinic, and writing while his students wrote during the writing clinic are all teacher-writer characteristics (Whitney, 2017).

Second, Deva considered herself a "good writer," whose writerly voice evolved across the semester to advocate for herself and her own children. Whitney (2017) states teacher-writers advocate for children in their writing. Perhaps Deva's writing experience reflects more of a parent-writer stance than a teacher-writer stance. Deva contemplated the audience of her self-healing narrative to whom she first considered writing to her children as follows:

> I'm trying to narrow it down to one audience. My topic for my narrative is my impending divorce and the events throughout the years that led me to take the steps I am taking. As for my audience, I initially wanted it to be my children to serve as an explanation for them when they get older, but if I did that, I'd be limited in the amount of details I'd want to

divulge. I'm still contemplating who my audience will be. I'm thinking as I'm writing this that I may want my audience to be my husband. It would be so therapeutic for me to write this to him, even if I don't ever show it to him.

(Deva, Electronic Writing Conference, Fall 2017)

Deva chose her audience, her soon-to-be ex-husband, as the following excerpt highlights:

> *Letter to my (soon-to-be-ex) husband*
> *Our daughter comes into the room, her phone held to her ear, and looks fearlessly into your angry red face.*
> *"I live at [1234 Woodlawn] and my dad is beating the crap out of my mom," she says calmly.*
> *You stop. The police arrive so quickly, I hardly had time to tie my hair back. ...*
> *I was so proud of our daughter. You, on the other hand, still hold it against her to this day. She stopped you. She stood up to you in ways I had never dared. How could my child be so strong with me as an example? I am so inspired by her. She is my hero.*
> *The day I finally decided to end it, you were home ... my phone rings. It's our daughter ... "Dad hit me! He punched me!" she cries, pleading for me to come home fast ...*
> *I calmly ask our daughter to take her siblings to the car. Once they're safe, I say to you the words I should have said the day after our daughter was born and you beat me to the floor. Words I should have said the day you pushed me down the stairs when I was eight months pregnant with our second daughter. Words I should have, could have, but didn't say to you on countless occasions of abuse.*
> *"You can leave on your own or you can leave in handcuffs."*
> *You have never seen me this sure before.*
> *I'm capable.*
> *You underestimate me.*

Due to our writing community's exploration of domestic violence, I wondered if Deva's experiences with the writing community empowered her choice to file for divorce during the semester. She confirmed my wondering through member checking. As a teacher-writer, I believe my influence played a small role in her topic selection. When I modeled my process for choosing an argument topic, I modeled freewriting, which took me to a childhood memory of domestic violence my mother experienced. For the next mini lesson, I modeled revising the freewrite into an anecdote to hook readers into an argument piece about domestic violence, a topic evident in Deva's narrative and Jowan Nabha's argument writing. I believe my choice to address a too-often silenced topic inspired Jowan to write about the topic, the third illustration.

Jowan detailed a controversial topic through her argument piece titled: Patriarchal Norms & Gender/Spousal Roles Influence How Arab Families View Domestic Violence. I also provided her with feedback on her first draft. After the course, I received the following email from her:

> I am writing to let you know that I have finally made a decision to submit my argumentative piece in hopes it will be published. I'm still waiting for a response. Wish me luck! I think if this one falls through I will try another source. I really want my voice to be heard in regards to this topic.
>
> (May 6, 2018)

Her email shows an anticipation of rejection. She received a revise and resubmit request from the *Arab America* publication, but at the time of this writing, Jowan has not revised the piece. Interestingly, a few months prior to submitting her argument to *Arab America*, she shared during her post-course interview her insecurities with writing:

> I would say I am a sometimes reluctant writer … I don't write with confidence a lot of times … I need a goal when I'm writing …The argumentative paper that I just wrote was definitely a positive because of like the feedback I guess I wasn't expecting … I feel like I want to write more like it's something now that okay I have motivation on that level but there's still like insecurities.
>
> (Jowan Nabha, Post-Course Interview, February 9, 2018)

I invited Jowan to be a guest blogger on my website, the reason I invited her to waive her anonymity for this research study. I knew from her post-course interview Jowan wanted to start a blog, so I was not surprised to receive her blogpost the next morning detailing her first experience submitting for publication; an excerpt follows:

> I want my voice to be heard. I'm tired of waiting for someone else to tell a story similar to mine when I am more than able to share with the world my story and perhaps have someone relate to me. With the knots in my stomach and a coffee cup in my hand, I clicked send and put myself out

there for the world to judge ... even with rejection, good things will come out of this piece.

(May 7, 2018, http://danielledefauw.com/2018/05/07/the-power-of-a-teacher-writers-voice/)

That summer, she wrote blogposts for #TeachWriteChat blog (https://teachwritechat.blogspot.com/) and joined an online writer's workshop through the site.

Jowan continues to grow as a teacher-writer willing to share her work with an audience. No longer a reluctant writer upon hitting send on her email, she is determined to publish her work. Publication is a validation to her teacher-writer's voice she uses to empower her readers (Whitney, 2017). Her final post-course interview response highlights the writing-course goal as she transferred her own experiences as a teacher-writer choosing to achieve publication despite her writing insecurities: "I definitely will encourage my students to write without fear even though I have a lot of insecurities." Her personal experiences will provide her future students with a strong motivator when she shares how she faced her writing insecurities.

These preservice teachers wrote with teacher-writer hearts, yet they did not self-identify as teacher-writers during the course. As Figure 0.1. illustrates, the two smaller gears begin moving as preservice teachers participate in writing workshop during our in-person sessions. Preservice teachers make writerly choices and demonstrate many teacher-writer strategies, even though the majority of them never self-identify as a teacher-writer. I question at which point in our careers educators may self-identify as a teacher-writer. I learned about teacher-writer identity during my Master's degree program as a third-grade teacher. Preservice teachers do not self-identify as teachers yet because they are learning to become teachers. Like building blocks, self-identification begins with seeing oneself as a teacher and a writer before contemplating the notion of self-identity as a teacher-writer.

References

Araujo, J., Szabo, S., Raine, L., & Wickstrom, C. (2014). Bridging the stories of experience: Preservice teachers revise their thinking about writing and the teaching of writing in an undergraduate literacy course. In S. Vasinda, S. Szabo, & R. Johnson (Eds.), *37th yearbook of the Association of Literacy Educators and Researchers* (pp. 225–238). Association of Literacy Educators and Researchers.

Atwell, N. (1998). *In the middle: New understandings about writing, reading, and learning.* Boynton/Cook Publishers, Inc.

Barnard, I. (2014). *Upsetting composition commonplaces.* Utah State University Press.

Bennett, S. (2007). *That workshop book: New systems and structures for classrooms that read, write, and think.* Heinemann.

Bergmann, J., Sams, A., & Gudenrath, A. (2015). *Flipped learning for English instruction*. International Society for Technology in Education.
Calkins, L.M. (2006). *Units of study for teaching writing: Grades 3-5*. FirstHand.
Colby, S.A., & Stapleton, J.N. (2006). Preservice teachers teach writing: Implications for teacher educators. *Reading Research and Instruction, 45*(4), 353–376. doi:10.1080/19388070609558455
Conference on College Composition and Communication. (1989/2013/2015). *Principles for the postsecondary teaching of writing*. http://www.ncte.org/cccc/resources/positions/postsecondarywriting
Cramer, R.L., & Cramer, B.B. (1975). Writing by imitating language models. *Language Arts, 52*, 1011–1015.
Cutler, L., & Graham, S. (2008). Primary grade writing instruction: A national survey. *Journal of Educational Psychology, 100*(4), 907–919.
DeFauw, D.L. (2016). Fourth-grade students' perceptions of their teacher as a writer. *Michigan Reading Journal, 48*(3), 7–16.
DeFauw, D.L., & Smith, M. (2016). Writing for an authentic audience – One teacher-writer's narrative journey. *Teaching/Writing: The Journal of Writing Teacher Education, 5*(1), 104–126. http://scholarworks.wmich.edu/wte/vol5/iss1/7/
Dorfman, L.R., & Cappelli, R. (2009). *Nonfiction mentor texts: Teaching informational writing through children's literature K-8*. Stenhouse Publishers.
Dorn, L.J., & Soffos, C. (2001). *Scaffolding young writers: A writer's workshop approach*. Stenhouse Publishers.
Duke, N.K., Purcell-Gates, V., Hall, L.A., & Tower, C. (2006). Authentic literacy activities for developing comprehension and writing. *The Reading Teacher, 60*(4), 344–355. doi:10.1598/RT.60.4.4
Ede, L., & Lunsford, A. (1984). Audience addressed/audience invoked: The role of audience in composition theory and pedagogy. *College Composition and Communication, 35*(2), 155–171. doi:10.2307/358093
Elf, N. (2017). Taught by bitter experience: A timescales analysis of Amalie's development of writer identity. In T. Cremin & T. Locke (Eds.), *Writer identity and the teaching and learning of writing* (pp. 183–199). Routledge. doi:10.4324/9781315669373
Englert, C.S., Raphael, T.E., Fear, K.L., & Anderson, L.M. (1988). Students' metacognitive knowledge about how to write informational texts. *Learning Disability Quarterly, 11*(1), 18–46. doi:10.2307/1511035
Getz, S. (2018, January 29). *Mentor texts for teaching argument writing*. National Council of Teachers of English. https://www2.ncte.org/blog/2018/01/mentor-texts-teaching-argument-writing/
Graham, S., & Perin, D. (2007). *Writing next: Effective strategies to improve writing of adolescents in middle and high schools*. Alliance for Excellent Education.
Graham, S., Harris, K.R., & Santangelo, T. (2015). Research-based writing practices and the common core: Meta-analysis and meta-synthesis. *The Elementary School Journal, 115*(4), 498–522. doi:10.1086/681964
Graves, D.H. (2004). What I've learned from teachers of writing. *Language Arts, 82*(2), 88–94.
Heard, G. (2002). *The revision toolbox: Teaching techniques that work*. Heinemann.

Herrington, A., & Herrington, J. (2006). What is an authentic learning environment. In A. Herrington & J. Herrington (Eds.), *Authentic learning environments in higher education* (pp. 1–14). Information Science Publishing.

Herrington, J., Reeves, T.C., & Oliver, R. (2014). Authentic learning environments. In J.M. Spector, M.D. Merrill, J. Elen, & M J. Bishop (Eds.), *Handbook of research on educational communications and technology* (pp. 410–412). Springer. doi:10.4018/978-1-59140-594-8.ch001

Hillocks, G., Jr. (1984). What works in teaching composition: A meta-analysis of experimental treatment studies. *American Journal of Education, 93*(1), 133–170. doi:10.1086/443789

Hooper, S.R., Wakely, M.B., de Kruif, R.E.L., & Swartz, C.W. (2006). Aptitude-treatment interactions revisited: Effect of metacognitive intervention on subtypes of written expression in elementary school students. *Developmental Neuropsychology, 29*(1), 217–241.

Ivanič, R. (2006). Language learning and identification. In R. Kiely, P. Rea-Dickens, H. Woodfield, & G. Clibbon (Eds.), *Language, culture and identity in applied linguistics* (pp. 7–29). Equinox.

Kaufman, D.K. (2009). A teacher educator writes and shares: Student perceptions of a publicly literate life. *Journal of Teacher Education, 60*(3), 338–350. doi:10.1177/0022487109336544

Lane, B. (1993). *After the end: Teaching and learning creative revision*. Heinemann.

Lave, J., & Wenger, E. (1991). *Situated learning: Legitimate peripheral participation*. Cambridge University Press. doi:10.1017/CBO9780511815355

Lindblom, K. (2004). Writing for real. *English Journal, 94*(1), 104–108.

Lindblom, K. (2015, July 27). *School writing vs. authentic writing. Teachers, profs, parents: Writers who care: A blog advocating for authentic writing instruction*. https://writerswhocare.wordpress.com/2015/07/27/school-writing-vs-authentic-writing/

Lloyd-Jones, S. (2019). *Look! I wrote a book! (And you can too!)*. [Illustrated by N. Layton]. Schwartz and Wade Books.

Phillips, D.K., & Larson, M.L. (2015). *Becoming a teacher of writing in elementary classrooms*. Routledge.

Portalupi, J., & Fletcher, R.J. (2004). *Teaching the qualities of writing: Ideas, design, language, presentation*. Firsthand.

Premont, D.W., Young, T.A., Wilcox, B., Dean, D., & Morrison, T.G. (2017). Picture books as mentor texts for 10th grade struggling writers. *Literacy Research and Instruction, 4*, 290–310. doi:10.1080/19388071.2017.1338803

Pytash, K.E., Edmondson, E., & Tait, A. (2014). Using mentor texts for writing instruction in high school economics class. *Social Studies Research and Practice, 9*(1), 95–106.

Rylant, C. (1985). *The relatives came*. [Illustrated by S. Gammell]. Bradbury Press.

Sayre, A.P. (2001). *Dig, wait, listen: A desert toad's tale*. [Illustrated by B. Bash]. Greenwillow Books.

Sayre, A.P. (2010). *Turtle, turtle, watch out!* [Illustrated by A. Patterson]. Charlesbridge.

Shanahan, T. (2015). Common core state standards: A new role for writing. *The Elementary School Journal, 115*(4), 464–479. doi:10.1086/681130

Stolarek, E.A. (1994). Prose modeling and metacognition: The effect of modeling on developing a metacognitive stance toward writing. *Research in the Teaching of English, 28*(2), 154–174.

Wenger, E., McDermott, R., & Snyder, W.M. (2002). *Cultivating communities of practice: A guide to managing knowledge.* Harvard Business School Press.

Whitney, A. (2017). Developing the teacher-writer in professional development. In T. Cremin & T. Locke (Eds.), *Writer identity and the teaching and learning of writing* (pp. 67–80). Routledge. doi:10.4324/9781315669373

Wiggins, G. (2009). Real-world writing: Making purpose and audience matter. *English Journal, 98*(5), 29–37.

Woodson, J. (2004). *Coming on home.* [Illustrated by E.B. Lewis]. G.P. Putnam's Sons.

Part II
Applying Pedagogical Content Knowledge of Writing through Academic Service Learning

4 Teach Writing
Connecting with Students and Families through Writing Clinics

The school gym buzzes with excitement as elementary students gather to attend the writing clinic's first session. On a November Tuesday afternoon around 3:40 pm, I connect each preservice teacher with one to three elementary students. The groups collect new composition notebooks, hardcover blank books, crayons, and pencils and parade to one of three classrooms the principal and teachers have invited us to use. Preservice teachers implement their mini lesson: model nonfiction writing using their own mentor text created during the first month of the flipped writing methodology course. Like their preservice teachers, students begin their writing process to create an informational/explanatory piece over the next four to six sessions. Families join the students for the final session to celebrate the students' writing processes completed throughout the writing program.

To prepare for the writing clinic, preservice teachers participate in writing workshop during the first half of the semester. They write informational/explanatory pieces to teach elementary students content (e.g., math, science, or social studies). Preservice teachers transfer their learning during the second half of the semester as they apply (PCKW) through the afterschool writing clinic scheduled conveniently during the in-person class time as Nadia shared:

> I like how we had the chance to work with a student one-on-one. I know we had to write a few essays in the beginning ... I like how we had a chance to make our own and put ourselves in the child's perspective ... I remember mine was like Sally's Middle School survival kit. I got to put myself into a child's perspective. I actually like that and then we actually had the chance to implement it and teach it to the child. So, we took what we learned in the first half and then taught it to the child. That's important. That's what I came here to learn is how to be a teacher. Not just to

write papers on how to be a teacher. Actually, do it. So then when we graduate and actually become teachers it's not as shocking or scary.

(Nadia, Post-Course Interview, May 22, 2018)

Threaded throughout this chapter, preservice teachers' reflections highlight how they applied PCKW through the writing clinic. The next sections detail how the writing clinic supports preservice teachers' development. Next, I detail benefits and challenges of hosting writing clinics on or off campus. Detailed steps for implementing writing clinics for families are provided, including: (a) tutor elementary students in writing for four to six weeks, (b) invite families to join during the same time to share home-school literacy strategies, (c) host a writing clinic celebration, and (d) connect families with a published children's book author.

Writing Clinic Content

Preservice teachers support students' nonfiction writing development during the writing clinic because the CCSS require informational/explanatory and argument writing as two of the three genres K-12 teachers are required to teach. Also, using nonfiction picture books as mentor texts, I find writing informational/explanatory genres creates myriad opportunities to blend nonfiction and fiction writing strategies such as *showing-versus-telling* details, using narrative anecdotes to hook readers, and writing about a topic using the power of one. For example, in the following excerpt, Hannah used the power of one in her informational/explanatory piece as the reader follows a cat's narrated morning-to-night routine as he interacts with his owner's rescue kittens:

> Making his way down the wooden hallway he perks his ears up to a slight noise in the distance. It's getting closer ... Zoom! Zoom! Zoom! He almost gets run down by the three foster kittens his mom brought home. They run right by the big white cat. He decides he needs to investigate where they are going. When he reaches the bedroom, he tip-toes around the corner. He sees the three kittens running up and down the room passing around the purple, scaly, toy fish. He decides they have too much energy for him right now seeing how it is getting close to nap time.

Additionally, Hannah posted facts about cats in the margins such as "Cats have 32 muscles in their ears." Hannah used her informational/explanatory piece as a mentor text with her students during the writing clinic's sessions.

I invite preservice teachers to use the same mini lessons for the writing clinic that I teach them throughout the course's writing workshop sessions. I encourage preservice teachers to write their own lesson plans, especially if they have prior experience with lesson planning, but I have found that providing at least the first lesson for the writing clinic eases preservice teachers' anxieties about the Academic Service Learning (ASL) experience. Also, because preservice teachers have experienced the lessons as writers themselves, they are better prepared to teach the content.

The second through fifth writing-clinic sessions include different lesson plans preservice teachers tailor to their students' needs. Sometimes, preservice teachers use one lesson plan across sessions. For example, some preservice teachers teach the Read, Reread, List, Compose (RRLC) lesson with their students (Kettel & DeFauw, 2018); this lesson teaches students to create a bulleted list of keywords as they read. Each bullet must have three or fewer words. Then, students summarize the content using only their bulleted lists to paraphrase content. Some preservice teachers use mini-lesson examples we complete during writing workshop. The final session's 15-minute lesson addresses listening and speaking skills to encourage audience participation during the writing clinic celebration.

The data in Table 0.2 show preservice teachers transferred their learning from their in-person writing workshop experiences to the teaching they provided their students in the writing clinic. The overall transfer category was evident in 594 references, 420 of which were sub-coded within data referencing the writing clinic. Through the writing clinic, preservice teachers transferred course content related to teaching writer's craft to the students per the following categories with the number of references in brackets: (a) mentor texts [108], revising [80], adding details [40], idea generation [40)], graphic organizers [33], RRLC strategy [31], word choice [24], technology [19], organization [16], genre study [14], editing [12], and dictating [3]. Aside from the graphic-organizers category, the data are not surprising since the writing clinic is designed to facilitate preservice teachers' transfer of learning, especially since most preservice teachers use lesson plans during the writing clinic that I implement in the writing workshop, as one preservice teacher stated in the anonymous course evaluation: "She also had us using everything we learned in the classroom to teach young students how to write like authors during our service learning at the writing clinic."

For this course, I do not model using graphic organizers, yet many preservice teachers discover their students need such scaffold supports. Also, preservice teachers may need these scaffolds to help guide students' idea generation and organization as seven participants, as detailed in their field note journals, utilized graphic organizers they created or downloaded from the Internet including Ryder's sentence-variety worksheets, Shannon's backward triangle graphic organizer for narrowing a topic, and Harper's organization worksheet and KWL chart. The data show two participants modeled how to complete the graphic organizers. For example, Andrea modeled how to use a detail chart she created to help her student "formulate his thoughts in a constructive manner" and sequence his football-topic details. She stated, "It's easier for him to look at his information on a chart and then write the piece around his details." Andrea noted they spent one session reading books and completing the chart. She questioned her student's progress: "It took much longer to find the details than I thought and we didn't get to begin our writing. I should have put aside more time for finding details." She also stated, "The detail chart did work, but it would've been a lot better if it had more details." Deva modeled in her writer's notebook how to use a brainstorming graphic organizer. Her student was able to "create a mind map based on his interests. What didn't work were the subtopics in the mind map. [Her student] was not able to come up with subtopics and nearly gave up." To support her student, Deva provided subtopic examples her student threaded into an outline but he "still needed support in the aspect of what details were important and how to organize [the] details."

Preservice teachers who connected reading and writing instruction used graphic organizers. For the first writing-clinic session, Ari required his student to complete a concept map, listing four facts from Stevie Wonder's life per a read aloud. Roberta created idea maps, storyboard worksheets, and animal research handouts to support her students' writing progress. As a published children's book author, her lessons reflected her experience with creating storyboards.

Jared used graphic organizers as a preservice and student teacher. During the writing clinic, Jared provided a brainstorming web worksheet and a six-question worksheet to help his students elaborate on their topics. As a student teacher, he wanted to help students transfer graphic-organizer use:

> When it comes to writing, I kind of like to learn more like how you introduce it, and how you can get kids to work with it, and use it afterwards. Rather than just like, this is the organizer, we're going to fill it out one-time type thing, and then like, leave it alone.
>
> (Jared, Student-Teaching Interview, December 15, 2016)

Jared's experience supports my bias with using graphic organizers as worksheets.

Too often as a literacy coach, I saw teachers use graphic organizers as a worksheet versus as a tool to mediate effective writing. For example, the five-paragraph essay is often supported through graphic organizers. For future sessions, I will model how to draw simple graphic organizers in my writer's notebook. Preservice teachers and students should not perceive graphic organizers as worksheets, but as tools they can draw in their writer's notebooks to support their writing processes.

The data force me to question the absence of graphic-organizer instruction in the course. A quarter of the participants used graphic organizers and more preservice teachers may have used graphic organizers but never included them in their lesson plans. I noted preservice teachers' using graphic organizers in my field notes. Regardless, the data show a needed course change: model and provide module content on graphic organizers' role in the writing process.

University-Hosted Writing Clinic Versus Afterschool Writing Clinic

Although writing clinics are beneficial no matter where they are held, in this section, I will highlight what my experiences have taught me regarding writing clinics hosted at the University or a local school. I have facilitated six writing clinics in different elementary schools and university contexts, three of which included parent-writer sessions. Writing clinics implemented at an elementary school following dismissal proved to be ideal.

The first two writing clinics were hosted once a week from 6:15 pm–7:30 pm because the course was scheduled from 6:00 pm–8:45 pm:

- The Winter 2013 writing clinic was hosted on campus; transportation and attendance were a challenge for families. Only 8 of the 15 families the principal and third-grade teachers invited attended the 6-week writing clinic: 6 African Americans, 1 Hispanic/Latino, and 1 European American. From these 8 families, 10 students worked with the three preservice and two inservice teachers enrolled in the course.
- The Fall 2014 writing clinic was hosted at an elementary school where the late session, 6:15 pm–7:30 pm, proved problematic for family routines (e.g., bedtime, dinnertime, etc.) even though transportation issues were alleviated. Low enrollment and absenteeism were a challenge despite refreshments being offered and a dedicated teacher who connected with the families in her school throughout the collaboration. All 120 third-grade students and their families were invited; 16 students attended the six-session writing clinic: 12 African American, 2 European American, and 2 Hispanic/Latino. These 16 students worked with 21 preservice and 4 inservice teachers enrolled in the course who co-taught and/or attended the family sessions.

Although attendance certainly impacted the writing clinic's quality, preservice teachers co-taught as needed, observed one another, or participated in the family sessions; but ideally, each preservice teacher needed at least one student to tutor. Ari stated:

> It was unfortunate that some of my ... peers did not have the opportunity that was granted to me. The support structure that was present in the classrooms to aid at any moment was phenomenal. Although some of my fellow classmates did not know if they were going to have a student one week or none at all, watching and observing these experiences turned out to be quite beneficial. They had the chance to witness real collaborations between students, teachers, parents, and the community.
>
> (Ari, Post-Course Interview, February 10, 2015)

Students who attended the writing-clinic sessions seemed motivated as the following two quotes suggest:

> Maybe something happened, which caused [my student] to not be able to attend the sessions anymore. We don't know. It is just very unfortunate that she wasn't able to finish her piece because everything was going so well, and she seemed so excited about it and looked forward to attending the clinic.
>
> (Carly, Post-Course Interview, February 16, 2015)

> [My student] also wondered why she had to wait a whole week to come back to the writing clinic ... She did not have an opportunity to actually write her story, but she still chose to share her process with the [writing clinic celebration] audience and share the idea for what she plans to write.
>
> (Brenda, Post-Course Interview, February 16, 2015)

In collaboration with the school that hosted the Fall 2014 writing clinic, we determined afterschool hours would be ideal for the writing clinic. In order to change the schedule for the flipped writing methodology writing course from a once-a-week evening course to a two-times-a-week afternoon course, I applied for ASL designation and argued preservice teachers needed to take the course at the same time we could offer the afterschool writing clinic at the local elementary school, per the school's request. The course did not run in Fall 2015 as I was on family leave to care for my newborn. For Fall 2016, the school informed me in May they could not host the writing clinic due to budget cuts.

I contacted another principal for the Fall 2016 semester. Unfortunately, the principal canceled the writing clinic the day before the first session. The cancellation shocked me as monthly communication during the previous spring and biweekly communication that Fall remained positive. I believe low enrollment motivated the principal's choice. I quickly made arrangements (e.g., IRB amendments, site permission, etc.) to run the writing clinic on campus. Through our listserv, I invited families to enroll their third-, fourth-, or fifth-grade students on a first-come, first-served basis. My inability to fulfill the myriad email requests to attend the writing clinic pained me. Because eight preservice teachers enrolled in the course, we could enroll only 24 students in the ten-session writing clinic. We hosted the writing clinic on campus from 3:45 pm –4:45 pm.

A teacher who received the Fall 2016 email invitation contacted me. She wondered if the writing clinic could be hosted at her school. In collaboration with her principal, the school hosted the writing clinic during their afterschool program beginning Fall 2017 and continuing to the present. Transportation is easier for families and the elementary school has ownership. With the principal's and teachers' support, the writing clinic is a win-win for everyone involved. The only drawback to an afterschool writing clinic is that families do not participate in the family sessions; they pick up their students at the end of each session. As the list below highlights, collaborating with the same school has increased yearly participation:

- For Fall 2017, 16 third-grade students attended the six-session writing clinic and worked with 21 preservice teachers. Preservice teachers co-taught as needed.
- For Fall 2018, 25 third-grade students attended the 5-session writing clinic and worked with 24 preservice teachers.
- For Fall 2019, 36 third-, fourth-, and fifth-grade students (12 students per grade) attended the 5-session writing clinic and worked with 20 preservice teachers. Many of the fourth- and fifth-grade students participated previously in the writing clinic.

Implementing a University-Hosted Writing Clinic

To host a writing clinic at a University, the following suggestions may apply:

- Seek permission to host the writing clinic.
- Seek Internal Review Board approval.
- Meet University requirements regarding children on campus.
- Secure a location and parking.
- Ensure preservice teachers' clearances are on file (e.g., criminal background check, blood borne pathogens training).
- Invite individuals to the writing clinic through collaboration with a local school. Request the principal and teachers invite students in one grade level to the writing clinic. When you cannot collaborate with a school, you may provide an open invitation via email to create a

registration-until-filled opportunity. Requiring tuition is an option, too, but I prefer to offer free writing clinics to increase access.
- Plan to have one to three students per preservice teacher. I prefer small groups of three students to support social interactions and alleviate absenteeism challenges.
- Prepare signage to navigate families to the writing clinic's location. For many families, the writing clinic may be their first experience on a college campus. For the first session, I have placed preservice teachers strategically from the parking lot to the writing clinic's location.
- Provide students with a writer's notebook, pencils, crayons, and a hardcopy blank book for the final copy.
- Invite families to sign any required paperwork.
- I require families to stay on campus. Although not required, I invite families to attend family sessions.
- Families have not asked to attend the writing clinic with their students. If a family member requested to attend, I would select the student's preservice teacher thoughtfully.

Implementing an Elementary School Writing Clinic

To host a writing clinic at an elementary school, the following suggestions may apply:

- Seek permission to host the writing clinic at a local school with the principal's and teachers' support.
- Seek Internal Review Board approval.
- Ensure preservice teachers' clearances, those required by the University and the school, are on file (e.g., criminal background check, blood borne pathogens training).
- Tour the location. If you host the writing clinic after school, contemplate traffic and parking. In our context, preservice teachers arrive five minutes after dismissal once buses and families have left.
- Ask the principal and teachers to invite one to three elementary students (grade level of school's choice) per preservice teacher to the writing clinic.
- Provide students with a writer's notebook, pencils, crayons, and a hardcopy blank book.
- Invite families to sign any required paperwork.
- Families may attend informational sessions you provide, but many of them do not pick students up until the writing-clinic session ends.
- Provide principal and teachers with thank you notes following the writing clinic.

Implementing Parent-Writer Groups

While preservice teachers lead the tutoring sessions with elementary students through University-hosted or local-school writing clinics, I lead parent-writer groups as informational sessions for families to support home/school literacy connections. Each family session consists of (a) picture book read alouds, (b) modeled writing, (c) time to write, (d) time to share, and (e) encouragement for transferring strategies to home contexts. Similarly, Kelly (2006) facilitated "Family Scribe Groups [which] are made up of families who meet, in order to write, with the guidance of one or more facilitators" (p. 7). Table 4.1 provides steps for implementing parent-writer groups. Table 4.2 details twenty books that provide effective writing prompts for families to explore in their family dialogue journals (Allen et al., 2015); see DeFauw (2017) for 11 additional suggestions.

During a typical parent-writer group session, families listen to me read aloud a picture book, such as *The Quiet Place* by Sarah Stewart (2012), illustrated by David Small. I model writing in response to one of the following prompts: (a) describe your own quiet place, (b) list your favorite words, (c) share stories of creations you or your students created with boxes, (d) write a letter to a special family member, or (e) write about your experiences learning a new language or moving to a new place. Families select one of the prompts for me to model. Unprepared, I model writing's messiness. Most recently, families asked me to write about my own quiet place. I modeled how I described quiet places I've enjoyed across my lifespan such as Houghton Lake's shore and the willow trees' shade at Crampton Park. I invite families to freewrite

Table 4.1 Steps for Implementing Parent-Writer Groups

1. Schedule parent-writer group sessions.
2. Select picture books, novel excerpts, poems, essays, or magazine articles to connect with families.
3. Identify a writing prompt for each text that connects to family dynamics.
4. Read aloud to the families, modeling effective prosody.
5. Share the writing prompt(s) related to the read aloud.
6. Model a 2- to 5-minute freewrite in response to the prompt, making connections to your own family.
7. Invite parent-writers to respond to the prompt through 5- to 15-minute freewrites.
8. Continue to add to your piece, silently, while the parent-writers write.
9. Ask parent-writers to pair/share their writing and then invite volunteers to share whole group.
10. Remind parent-writers to share their writing with their students.
11. Invite parent-writers to read aloud to their children and then determine a prompt to write in response to the text's content. Parent-writers and students can determine these prompts together and conduct shared or independent written responses.

Table 4.2 Books and Writing Prompts to Use with Families

Book	Summary	Writing Prompt
Arnoldo, M. (2018). *Little brothers & little sisters*. Owlkids Books Inc.	Younger siblings strive to keep up with older siblings, allowing for special memories.	Share sibling stories.
Bolts, M. (2007). *Those shoes*. [Illustrated by N.Z. Jones]. Candlewick Press.	Jeremy and Grandma search thrift stores for the brand shoes everyone is wearing. Jeremy buys a pair that does not fit and discovers the gift of giving.	Share stories of your family's needs or wants.
Bunting, E. (2000). *The memory string*. Houghton Mifflin.	Laura has a special memory string that is laced with buttons to remind her of her family. She is comforted when Stepmom finds a lost button.	Share memories of someone you love for each button you draw.
Cohn, A. (2003). *Firsts*. Accord Publishing.	A seven-year-old child highlights childhood's firsts.	Write one detail for each year of your child's life.
Gravett, E. (2013) *Again!* Simon & Schuster Books.	Cedric, the little dragon, begs his mother to reread a book. Cedric's frustration explodes when his mother falls asleep.	Share memories of your child's incessant pleas to reread books.
Hest, A. (2004). *Kiss good night*. [Illustrated by A. Jeram]. Candlewick Press.	A little bear loves his mama, especially when she forgets bedtime-routine details.	Detail changes in bedtime routines.
Hoffman, M. (2002). *The colour of home*. [Illustrated by K. Littlewood]. Penguin Putnam Books.	First-grader Hassan, entering school in America after leaving a war-torn country, cannot speak English. He tells his story through art.	Detail your family's journey and the sacrifices made to live in America.
Lovell, P. (2001). *Stand tall, Molly Lou Melon*. [Illustrated by D. Catrow]. G.P. Putnams.	Molly Lou Melon has an uncanny ability to turn her mistakes and faults into great accomplishments.	Detail your child's strengths.
Mack, J. (2013). *The things I can do*. The Roaring Book Press.	Jeff details the things he can do independently.	Detail things you can do with your children that will change as they grow.
Pak, S. (1999). *Dear Juno*. [Illustrated by S.K. Hartung]. Viking.	Juno and Grandma share letters and pictures to stay connected from Korea to the United States.	Write letters or draw pictures with family members.
Polacco, P. (1998). *Thank you, Mr. Falker*. Penguin Young Readers Group.	Patricia Polacco shares her personal experience meeting Mr. Falker, a fifth-grade teacher, who taught her how to read.	Share stories of favorite teachers or learning challenges.

(Continued)

Table 4.2 Continued

Book	Summary	Writing Prompt
Recorvits, H. (2003). *My name is Yoon.* [Illustrated by G. Swiatkowska]. Frances Foster Books.	Yoon's Korean name means Shining Wisdom. Because she prefers her name written in Korean, she misnames her papers until finally she introduces herself to her teacher.	Share stories behind children's names. Highlight teachers who have made a difference.
Rumford, J. (2008). *Silent music: A story of Baghdad.* Roaring Brook Press.	Ali loves calligraphy. He writes Arabic words to highlight his daily life.	Write letters with words and art to family members in your first language.
Smith, M.G. (2016). *My heart fills with happiness.* [Illustrated by J. Flett]. Orca Book Publishers.	Simple moments lived with loved ones fill a family's heart.	What fills your heart with happiness?
Soto, G. (1993). *Too many tamales.* [Illustrated by E. Martinez]. G.P. Putnam's Sons.	Maria loses Mama's ring while kneading masa for the Christmas celebration. Cousins gobble the tamales in search of Mama's ring.	Detail family traditions, stories of lost items, or moments children confessed to wrong-doing.
Stuve-Bodeen, S. (2010). *A small brown dog with a wet pink nose.* [Illustrated by L. Hunter]. Little Brown Books for Young Readers.	Playing a game with her parents about her imaginary dog, Bones, a young girl changes her parents' minds to say yes to a dog.	Write the story of bringing your pet home. Write about a time you or your child tricked one another.
Velasquez, E. (2001). *Grandma's records.* Walker & Company.	Eric Velasquez's memoir of time spent with his grandma highlights her love for music and her homeland.	Share songs you love.
Woodson, J. (2018). *The day you begin.* [Illustrated by R. López]. Nancy Paulsen Books.	A child learns that nothing in our lives is trivial. The stories we live and tell matter no matter how they may compare to others' experiences.	Find the extraordinary in the ordinary. Detail family routines and highlight what makes them special.
Yolen, J. (1987). *Owl moon.* Penguin Putnam Books for Young Readers.	A father and daughter walk together to discover the Great Horned Owl.	Share special family moments.
Zwillich, J. (2018). *Not 'til tomorrow, Phoebe.* [Illustrated by D. Holmes]. Owl kids Books.	Tomorrow feels far away. Phoebe wonders why Mom and her teacher can't let the fun happen today. Grandma helps her rest for tomorrow.	Share stories of anticipation.

for five minutes to a self-chosen prompt. Once families finish writing, I invite them to share with a partner before I ask for at least three volunteers to share whole group.

Overall, I encourage families to turn read alouds into writing opportunities completed through family dialogue journals (Allen et al., 2015). A family dialogue journal is a notebook family members share. My family's procedure is to write a letter to a family member and leave the composition notebook on that individual's pillow. Once the recipient writes back, they leave the family dialogue journal on the next person's pillow. Regardless of how family dialogue journals are used—supporting home/school connections, responding to questions or prompts, summarizing learning, sharing stories, or writing in response to picture books—they are invaluable tools for supporting family relationships, as Serene shared with families during the Fall 2014 family session:

> When I was younger me and my dad used to switch and read each other's journals ... My teachers used to always complain that I wasn't doing well in writing ... My dad said that we would practice more at home even though my dad wasn't really such a great writer ... He's like well we learn from each other. And we'd write ... he'd draw me pictures ... and we'd write to each other ... I didn't write too much or not at all until like after when I started writing with my dad in the journals ... I felt more comfortable writing.

In her writing history essay, Serene mentioned her "parents didn't finish middle school and are not fluent in English. They pushed and supported [her] siblings and [her] to keep learning and be successful in fulfilling the education they were not able to reach." Serene also stated in her writing history essay:

> I hold onto this and will pass it on to my children. I may not have had a great writing experience, but I am fortunate and thankful for the education I did receive. I want my children to have a better experience in writing than I did. In order for this to happen I need to learn strategies to inspire and encourage writing ... I want my own children to keep a personal writing journal.

For Serene, her phrase *my children* encapsulates her biological children and her future students.

Along with Serene, a few other preservice teachers joined the family sessions during the Fall 2014 semester due to low enrollment, which proved beneficial to the preservice teachers' professional development. For example, Carly stated the following in her field note journal:

Since the student only attended two of the clinic sessions, I was able to observe and participate in the parent sessions. ... The parents shared stories and advice and asked questions about how to help their child with literacy at home. Listening to the parents share their perspectives ... opened my eyes ... to collaborate with parents.

Carly also voiced the following professional goal in her eportfolio:

I hope to implement a writing clinic, similar to the one we held ... in order to hear families' stories about writing and incorporate those stories into my teaching.

Like Carly, teachers need to involve families in their writing curriculum (International Reading Association, 2002; McClay et al., 2012). This understanding must begin in preservice teacher preparation programs (Ferrara & Ferrara, 2005; McClay et al., 2012). Harper shared the following in her field note journal: "It was refreshing to work with parents because although I obviously love working with children, I don't feel we get enough experiences as preservice teachers to work with parents and families to build those essential partnerships." In her eportfolio, Harper continued her reflections as follows:

The most rewarding aspect of this class was being able to go out into the community. We worked at [an elementary school], and I was able to work with parents and families to help support them as they tackle writing instruction with their children. It was an amazing opportunity, as I gained familiarity and experience working with families and supporting them to build trusting partnerships that benefit the children. I was able to listen to the families as they stated their hopes and fears for their children and reach out to them to provide support and assistance. I have had many experiences working with students in practicums, volunteering, and employment, but working with the families was an additional aspect to my role as an educator that was valuable and will enable me to be the best teacher I possibly can. I hope I was able to provide some laughs, insight, and enjoyment to the family instruction sessions, and show the families how important it is to remain engaged in their child's education.

High-quality writing instruction needs to permeate students' lives in and outside of school. Students' first teachers—their families—must be supported to strengthen student writing development and, most importantly, family bonds as Ari stated in his eportfolio, "I became a more confident, enthusiastic writer through the guidance of my parents." Families are an intricate thread of their students' education, in and outside of school. Few families adamantly resist the opportunity to become more involved in their students' education (Sentz, 2011). My experience has taught me families want to be involved, but do not know, necessarily, how to help.

Many home-school literacy strategies parallel one another. Shockley et al. (1995) highlighted parallel practices to showcase how students engaged in similar literacy practices at home and at school, parallel practices that honored families' funds of knowledge (González et al., 2006). Through such parallel practices, families wrote about family stories they retold for their shared enjoyment (Shockley et al., 1995). Stillman (1989) encouraged families to engage in family writing projects to create a legacy for generations to cherish. Kelly (2006) emphasized "Family Scribe Groups write about what they know best: their own lives" (p. 7) and Family Scribe Groups may write group poems, share and write about artifacts or photographs, create artistic representations, or write letters to family members.

In addition to promoting family writing experiences at home, inviting families into the writing workshop in-person or virtually is also beneficial. Rhonda wanted to encourage families through modeled writing:

> I think we also need to model for the parents too. I think it's a big thing. I mean we model for the students on a day-to-day basis, but if you can't portray that to a parent then you're really not getting your lesson across. It's not going to be as effective because they don't see the meaning behind it ... have the adult perspective behind it as to why you're doing this and why it's important and why the student needs to be introduced to these different things.
>
> (Rhonda, Post-Course Interview, February 16, 2015)

Zurcher (2016) encouraged teachers to welcome family support in the writing workshop. Not only would families see the teacher model writing for students, but Zurcher encouraged inviting families to provide feedback during writing conferences in class. Additionally, Zurcher encouraged families to participate in family writing opportunities at home. Educators need to empower families with tools to promote students' academic success (Edwards, 2016). Through the writing clinic celebration, we celebrate such success.

Writing Clinic Celebration

Through the final writing-clinic session, we invite families to celebrate literacy with their students. Refreshments in hand, the families listen to the students read aloud their pieces, independently or with their preservice teachers beside them. Students' pieces demonstrate various writing-process stages.

Some students write their nonfiction piece in a hardcover blank book, with their final writing either typed or handwritten and their pages illustrated, while others read drafts or ideas from their writer's notebooks. The writing selections are rarely finished, but students seem motivated to finish their work at home with the provided resources. During the Fall 2019 semester, I discovered breaking the students into groups and presenting in one of three classrooms to a smaller audience was not as effective as presenting on the stage with the microphone to the entire audience in the cafeteria, the steps we took during the Fall 2017 and 2018 semesters.

Although a writing clinic celebration only requires families or an audience, twice I received grant support to offer an honorarium to a published children's book author to attend the writing clinic celebration. When such a guest attended during the Fall 2014 and Fall 2016 semesters, the following authors began the writing clinic celebration with a short presentation on their books before they handed the mic over to the students to share their own writing: (a) Matt Faulkner, author/illustrator of such books as *A Taste of Colored Water* published by Simon and Schuster and *The Monster Who Ate My Peas* published by Peachtree Publishing Company; and (b) Diane Bradley, author of the *Wilder Series*: *Wilder's Ghost*, *Wilder's Foe*, and *Wilder's Edge* published by Northstar Press. The authors remained in the audience while the students presented. Connecting families with published children's book authors motivates the audience to participate even more fully in the writing clinic celebration. Rhonda shared in her field note journal that she heard students talking to Mr. Faulkner afterwards about how they plan to be an author some day. I shared with her we never know what seed we plant that will be watered across a lifetime to change a family's legacy. I wonder how many students who have interacted with authors through the writing clinic and the Young Authors' Festival, as detailed in the next chapter, will become lifelong writers and maybe published children's book authors or illustrators.

References

Allen, J., Beaty, J., Dean, A., Jones, J., Mathews, S.S., McCreight, J., Schwedler, E., & Simmons, A.M. (2015). *Family dialogue journals: School-home partnerships that support student learning*. Teachers College Press.

DeFauw, D.L. (2017). Writing with parents in response to picture book read alouds. *Reading Horizons: A Journal of Literacy and Language Arts, 56*(2), 22–25. http://scholarworks.wmich.edu/reading_horizons/vol56/iss2/3/

Edwards, P.A. (2016). *New ways to engage parents: Strategies and tools for teachers and leaders, K-12*. Teachers College Press.

Ferrara, M.M., & Ferrara, P.J. (2005). Parents as partners raising awareness as a teacher preparation program. *The Clearing House, 79*(2), 77–82. doi:10.3200/TCHS.79.2.77-82

González, N., Moll, L., & Amanti, C. (2006). *Funds of knowledge: Theorizing practices in households, communities, and classrooms.* Lawrence Erlbaum. doi:10.4324/9781410613462

International Reading Association. (2002). *Family-school partnerships: Essential elements of literacy instruction in the United States: A position statement of the International Reading Association.* https://www.literacyworldwide.org/docs/default-source/where-we-stand/family-school-partnerships-position-statement.pdf?sfvrsn=904ea18e_6

Kelly, S.A. (2006). *Writing with families: Strengthening the home/school connection with family scribe groups.* Maupin House Publishing, Inc.

Kettel, R.P., & DeFauw, D.L. (2018). Paraphrase without plagiarism: Use RRLC (Read, Reread, List, Compose). *The Reading Teacher, 72*(2), 245–255. doi:10.1002/trtr.1697

McClay, J.K., Peterson, S.S., & Nixon, R. (2012). Parents and communities as partners in teaching writing in Canadian middle grades classrooms. *Middle School Journal, 44*(1), 44–52. doi:10.1080/00940771.2012.11461838

Sentz, L.W. (2011). *Write with me: Partnering with parents in writing instruction.* Routledge. doi:10.4324/9781315854427

Shockley, B., Michalove, B., & Allen, J. (1995). *Engaging families: Connecting home and school literacy communities.* Heinemann.

Stewart, S. (2012). *The quiet place.* [Illustrated by D. Small]. Farrar Straus Giroux.

Stillman, P.R. (1989). *Families writing.* Writer's Digest Books.

Zurcher, M.A. (2016). Partnering with parents in the writing classroom. *The Reading Teacher, 69*(4), 367–376. doi:10.1002/trtr.1421

5 Celebrate Writing

Connecting Students, Families, and Published Children's Book Authors and Illustrators through Writing Events

> *It is 8:30 am, Saturday morning in November when families visit the University of Michigan–Dearborn's Mardigian library for a free four-hour literacy event: the annual Young Authors' Festival. Pre-registered, families pick up their envelopes with session tickets, a map with highlighted breakout literacy sessions, and a gift bag filled with a writer's notebook, hardcover blank book, pencil, pen, sticky notes, stickers, crayons, and an anthology of the winning contest entries. Families snack on breakfast refreshments and take their seats by 9:00 am. Families listen to the author's one-hour presentation. Next, the 125 third-, fourth-, and fifth-grade students attend three thirty-minute breakout literacy sessions led by preservice teachers enrolled in a children's literature course. The parents stay in the whole-group area and participate in breakout sessions focused on home/school literacy connections. Parents peruse poster sessions preservice teachers enrolled in the flipped writing methodology course create. Then, writing contest winners in grades 3–5 receive their Barnes and Noble gift cards and read aloud excerpts from their entries placed first through third for each grade level and one grand-prize winner.*

The Young Authors' Festival (YAF) is another academic service learning (ASL) project completed through the flipped writing methodology course that includes multiple authentic learning opportunities to motivate writing: half-day literacy event, writing contest, and family resources (in-person and flipped). Through the YAF, students are motivated to read and write, families are provided with valuable strategies to implement at home, families connect with a published children's book author and/or illustrator, and preservice teachers experience the positive impact such authentic literacy opportunities create.

In this chapter, we will explore how writing festivals or literacy nights provide the following opportunities: (a) motivate elementary students to write through literacy breakout sessions, (b) empower families with home/school literacy strategies, and (c) connect families with published children's book authors and illustrators to inspire authentic writing. Literacy events can be as basic or formal as a budget allows. Finally, because the writing festival is one of two ASL opportunities provided through the flipped writing methodology course, I will address the second research question:

- How will preservice teachers apply pedagogical content knowledge of writing through academic service learning projects (e.g., third-grade writing clinic and Young Authors' Festival)?

Implementing a Half-Day Writing Festival

The YAF is a collaborative event shared between the University of Michigan–Dearborn's Mardigian Library and the Department of Education in the College of Education, Health, and Human Services. As co-chairs, three of us collaborate to procure funding sources, implement the YAF's schedule (detailed in Table 5.1), orchestrate details, and foster authentic instructional opportunities for preservice teachers (DeFauw et al., 2017, 2018). The 2013 YAF required a small budget, but publicity brought funding: grants and donations. The following details our honoraria:

- 2013: Author Carol Hagen, Illustrator Matt Faulkner, *The Night Henry Ford Met Santa*, Sleeping Bear Press, 2006
- 2014: Author Toni Buzzeo, 2013 Caldecott Honor Book, *One Cool Friend*, Dial Books, 2012

Table 5.1 2019 Young Authors' Festival Schedule

Time	Task
8:30 am–9:00 am	Check-in and light refreshments
9:00 am–9:50 am	Welcome and special guest presentation
9:50 am–10:00 am	Break and transition
10:00 am–10:30 am	Breakout session A
	Parent session read aloud
	Families peruse poster presentations
10:30 am–10:40 am	Break and transition
	Families continue to peruse poster presentations
10:40 am–11:10 am	Breakout session B
	Families continue to peruse poster presentations
11:10 am–11:20 am	Break and transition
11:20 am–11:50 am	Breakout session C
	Parent-writer session
11:50 am–12:00 pm	Break and transition
12:00 pm–12:30 pm	Writing contest award ceremony
12:30 pm–1:00 pm	Author/Illustrator book signing

- 2015: Author Gary D. Schmidt, 2008 Newbery Honor Book, *The Wednesday Wars*, Clarion Books, 2007
- 2016: Author Christopher Paul Curtis, 1996 Newbery Honor Book, *The Watsons Go To Birmingham—1963*, Yearling, 1995; and 2000 Newbery Winner, *Bud, Not Buddy*, Yearling, 1999
- 2017: Author/Illustrator Matt Faulkner, Illustrator of Kristen Remenar's *Groundhog's Dilemma*, Charlesbridge, 2015
- 2018: Graphic Novelist Mark Crilley, *Miki Falls* series, HarperCollins; *Brody's Ghost* series, Dark Horse Books; and the *Akiko* series, Delacorte Books for Young Readers
- 2019: Jean Alicia Elster, *The Colored Car*, Wayne State University Press, 2013
- 2020: Author Sarah Stewart and Illustrator David Small (Caldecott Winner and Honoree), *The Quiet Place*, Farrar, Straus and Giroux, 2012

Our YAF is free to the public due to financial support from the Mardigian Library, Department of Education, several other University departments, external organizations, community members, Barnes & Noble bookstore, and literacy-focused professional organizations. Festivals can be inexpensive. Author visits may be free. For example, Kate Messner's (n.d.) website, Authors Who Skype with Classes & Book Clubs (for free!), lists many authors and illustrators who offer free 20-minute Skype sessions. Local authors and/or new authors may be inexpensive.

The YAF is connected to the elementary educator preparation program for two Fall courses I teach to increase the authenticity of preservice teachers' coursework: a flipped writing methodology course and a children's literature course. Because preservice teachers are often enrolled in these two courses concurrently, I implemented changes in Fall 2018 to separate course content as detailed in Table 5.2. The following assignments remain consistent in the two courses: (a) preservice teachers in the children's literature course write and implement a read aloud lesson to help advertise the event, ideally using one of the honorarium's books, and lead the students' literacy breakout sessions during the YAF; (b) preservice teachers in the flipped writing methodology course evaluate the writing contest entries (since 2014) and provide parent-poster sessions that evolve into flipped resources posted to our YAF website (since 2018); and (c) preservice teachers write reflections concerning their YAF experiences.

To orchestrate the YAF as a required curricular component, I provide class time to prepare the breakout sessions. For example, since 2018, I have provided time for preservice teachers in the flipped writing methodology course to plan, in partnerships, breakout sessions for parents that preservice teachers share in-person during the YAF and then flip the following week into online

Table 5.2 Courses' Organization for Young Authors' Festival

YAF Year	Children's Literature Course	Flipped Writing Methodology Course
2013	Reading-focused 20-minute breakout session for students, repeated twice	Writing-focused 20-minute breakout session for students, repeated twice
2014–2016	Reading-focused 50-minute breakout session for students, repeated twice	Writing-focused 50-minute breakout session for students, repeated twice
2017	Parent resource shared through YAF website without flipped learning technology and reading-focused 50-minute breakout sessions for students, repeated twice	Writing-focused 50-minute breakout sessions for students, repeated twice
2018	Literacy-focused 50-minutee breakout sessions repeated twice	Parent resource shared through YAF website using flipped learning technology
2019–Present	Literacy focused 30-minute breakout session for students, repeated thrice	One literacy-focused, in-person parent-poster session, later flipped for YAF website

resources, independently, as detailed in Chapter 7 (e.g., Google folders with handouts, PowerPoint, screencast). Ultimately, partnerships create a poster presentation on any content they deem worthy of parents' time. Parents peruse the posters and receive a raffle ticket for each session they attend. The YAF committee raffles off a literacy-themed basket at the end of the YAF. During one to two class sessions following the YAF, preservice teachers learn to flip the parent-poster session's content into a screencast. The YAF committee selects the flipped resources posted to our parent YAF webpage, http://guides.umd.umich.edu/yafparents. Renee's eportfolio quote highlights her experience with the family resource requirement:

> This year my class also helped with the Young Authors' Festival. In this event, I was paired up with another student and we made an out-of-school activity that parents could do with their children to help them write more. This event was very different than the writing clinic as I had to learn to work with the parents rather than the students themselves. I also had to be prepared to answer the questions parents had for me. In the end, my partner and I were able to present our project both professionally and to a high educational standard. EXPS 298 has not only taught me how to be a better writer but I also learned how to be a better teacher to both the students and the parents as well.

Impact of YAF on Preservice Teachers' Transfer of Learning

Prior to Fall 2018, preservice teachers enrolled in the flipped writing methodology course led the literacy breakout sessions that presently only preservice teachers enrolled in the children's literature course lead. I provide time for preservice teachers in the children's literature course to plan, in small groups, a breakout session for students. The small-group, breakout-literacy-session task includes writing a blurb to advertise each session on the registration site. I stress high-quality, persuasive writing to entice families to sign their students up for the session. Preservice teachers write a lesson plan with their group and practice teaching the breakout sessions. Table 5.3 lists examples of breakout session topics for students that preservice teachers in the children's literature course teach.

Table 5.3 Examples of Breakout Session Topics

Breakout Session Title	Breakout Session Blurb
An Adventure Through Time	Be prepared to meet monsters, wizards, and other mythical creatures!
Drawing a Blank? Fill in and draw your own Mad Lib	Work with a partner to fill in, illustrate and explain a Mad Lib!
Match the Word to the Pic!	Work in groups to match words to their definition, opposite, and picture!
Pictures Tell Stories!	Create your own story from the quotes of Van Allsburg.
Tag, You're It!	Become an author as a team by creating a story!
Gobble, Gobble!	Share Thanksgiving traditions past and present.
Let's Make a Change	Step into the author's shoes to revise and act out a fairytale.
Postcard Palooza	Design your own postcard for someone special.
Creative Mind Flow	Pick descriptive words out of a bowl to write and illustrate a story.
The Journey of an Object	Personify an object and create its journey.
They all lived happily ever after … Or did they?	Switch up the ending of classic fairytales.
Memory Making with Comic Strips	Create your own comic strips about your favorite memory!
Thanksgiving Comic Books	Create comic books of thankfulness.
Become Your Own Illustrator	Draw your imagination while you listen to a story.
Think, Create, & Illustrate	Illustrate your own story about a family vacation.
Create Your Own Zootopia!	Imagine yourself as your favorite animal and write and illustrate.
Dear Future-Self	Write yourself a letter that you will open in the future!

Many preservice teachers enrolled in the flipped writing methodology course prior to Fall 2018 found the YAF's breakout sessions beneficial for motivating writing through genre exploration, modeling writing, and using mentor texts. Focused on motivating writing, Brenda stated in her eportfolio:

> The goal and purpose of this festival was to encourage children to develop a love of writing and show them that anyone is capable of becoming a writer if that is what they want to do … Participating in the Young Authors' Festival had a great impact on my skills as a writing teacher.

In her eportfolio, Brenda also reflected on encouraging students "to develop a love of writing and show them that anyone is capable of becoming a writer … If students have positive experiences with writing, such as those associated with the Young Authors' Festival, they will learn to enjoy writing."

Exploring genres to motivate writing, Andrea shared in her eportfolio that through her group's YAF lesson "students wrote themselves into their favorite TV show and put it into a comic strip form." Other preservice teachers explored genres not emphasized in the flipped writing methodology course, such as Ryder's YAF lesson focused on "helping students write their own fairy tale." Ryder detailed his group's procedure in his eportfolio and plans to transfer his learning to his future teaching experiences:

> First, we discussed with students common elements of fairy tales before reading them an excerpt from *Peter Pan*. Then, we helped them to fold books that they would write and/or illustrate their own fairy tales. The books many of these students created were quite impressive. This project helped to improve not only my lesson planning skills but also my ability to work with a group of people. It was extremely rewarding to see our hard work pay off and have the children create something uniquely them.

Some groups explored songwriting. For example, Travis' group, led by a ukulele player, "participated in musical storytelling [to] create a story through song … to teach the students to write to the beat of … *Row Row Row Your Boat*."

Two strategies preservice teachers transferred from in-person writing workshop sessions to the YAF breakout sessions included modeling and using mentor texts as evident in Roberta's and Brenda's YAF lesson. Roberta stated she, Brenda, and their other group members "modeled for the students using a big white board and collaborated on different ideas for the story. Doing this showed the students that their stories could go in many different directions." Roberta's eportfolio quote details transfer of her teacher-writer, writing workshop experiences to the YAF:

The Young Authors' Festival was significant to my development as a teacher-writer because it afforded me an opportunity to implement strategies and practices learned in the course. That is: the [YAF] provided me with an opportunity to use mentor texts and model writing during writing instruction with elementary students and it gave me additional experience in effectively conferencing with students about their writing.

Roberta's group also learned to select mentor texts purposefully as Roberta detailed in her eportfolio, strategies she transferred to the writing clinic:

There were some students who were advanced and others were in upper grades. Therefore, the mentor text that my group read aloud to students was on a lower reading level. For this reason, some of the students could have benefited from a more advanced text. This experience reinforced the importance of providing students with text choices and selecting leveled readers that are easy, moderate, and challenging for diverse student literacy needs … Collectively, my group agreed that we would incorporate leveled readers into mentor text selections for writer's workshops in the future. Still, it was a valuable insight for my group as a whole. Personally, following the Young Authors' Festival, I started to select leveled readers as mentor texts in [the writing clinic]. The students who participated in my ten-week tutoring sessions responded positively to having choices in writing mentor texts that were relevant to their writing tasks.

The YAF creates myriad learning opportunities for preservice teachers and families. As a committee, we are committed to offer the YAF for years to come due to its positive impact on our community. Maceo remembers a yearly writing festival he experienced in his school. Like Maceo shared in his writing history essay, we hope YAF participants will remember the YAF:

I was fortunate enough to have my school conduct a writing festival every year. In this festival, there would be different stations with different prompts and activities. It was fun to write with my peers and listen to all of the great stories that we would come up with. The writing festival also helped me write as I was able to learn new writing techniques from my peers and the leaders that led the workshop.

Writing festivals and afterschool writing events are memorable.

Implementing an Afterschool Writing Event

Afterschool literacy nights, a familiar educational context, facilitate writing events similar to writing festivals. I encourage preservice teachers to

Table 5.4 Afterschool Writing Event Schedule

Time	Task
5:30 pm–5:40 pm	Welcome families and offer refreshments.
5:40 pm–6:00 pm	Local expert, author, or reader shares their experiences.
6:00 pm–6:10 pm	Teacher leads a writing mini lesson (e.g., idea generation).
6:10 pm–6:40 pm	Families write.
6:40 pm–7:00 pm	Writers share in small groups and then volunteers share whole group.

implement, as inservice teachers, one-hour-and-a-half afterschool literacy nights where families listen to an author or a literacy expert and write. Families can write together following a teacher's mini lesson. For example, as a teacher models, families can read children's books together and write like the authors they read. Table 5.4 provides a schedule example and Table 4.2 details prompts to use with families. Another option includes inviting guest speakers to share their experiences as evident in the Authors Specialists Knowledge (ASK) program detailed in the next section.

Authors Specialists Knowledge (ASK) Program

Through the Authors Specialists Knowledge (ASK) program participants prepare an interview for an author or a specialist (Kettel, 1996). While reading a high-quality children's picture book or novel, students craft high-quality questions to ask the author or a specialist about the book's content through an in-person or virtual interview process. ASK programs are provided in the US through Two Way Interactive Connections in Education: https://twice.cc/. The following six steps may be followed to implement ASK programs:

1. Teacher or students choose a fiction or nonfiction book.
2. Teacher facilitates connections with the book's author or a specialist on the book's content.
3. Students and specialist or author read the book, independently.
4. Students write questions as they read.
5. Students are assigned questions to ask during the whole-group interview.
6. Students conduct the interview in-person or virtually.

Although not a component in the flipped writing methodology course, I remind preservice teachers to implement ASK programs as inservice teachers. All preservice teachers experience an ASK program in the children's literature course. To illustrate an ASK program, during the Fall 2017 semester, preservice teachers in the children's literature course read Deborah Ellis'

(2009) *The Bread Winner*, published by Groundwood Books, and interviewed Parwin Anwar, a refugee from Afghanistan who fled the 1984 Russian takeover. Although not part of the Taliban takeover in 1996 (per the novel's content), Mrs. Anwar explained the hardships children face during war. ASK programs provide opportunities to utilize a community's funds of knowledge (González et al., 2006). I encourage preservice teachers to begin with their future students' experiences to seek alignment to a book's content. For example, Cynthia Lord's (2006) *Rules*, published by Scholastic Press, provides a valuable book to explore sibling relationships when one sibling has Autism. Patricia Reilly Giff's (2004) *Pictures of Hollis Woods*, published by Yearling, provides a book to use when interviewing a class member or specialist who experienced the foster care system. Additionally, invite parents or local professionals within the community to be a specialist related to a book's content. The specialist reads the book and participates in-person or virtually for the interview. Authors shared with me they sometimes feel they need to read their own book to prepare for ASK programs because the preservice teachers' and students' questions dive deep into the book's content. Readers control ASK programs unlike most author visits.

Tips on Hosting Author Visits

Through the YAF experience, I encourage preservice teachers to connect families with published children's book authors. "The author visit is the basic backbone of building connections between readers (actual or potential) and writers" (Silverman, 2013, p. 27). Author visits, within educational contexts, provide positive effects on students that last a lifetime (Buzzeo, 2003). Some students experience a one-day, school-wide event where an author talks about their writing process used throughout a published book's creation (Hayes, 2010; Morgan, 2013). Author visits may be conducted in small-group writing sessions (Kahn, 2008) or critique groups (Follos, 2004). Some schools interact with the same author across an entire school year (DeFauw, 2018). Through such interactions, students learn the writing process is an authentic tool utilized in and outside of school (Gutman, 1997; Moynihan, 2009). Such interactions motivate students to write like published children's book authors (Morgan, 2013; Naslund & Jobe, 2005). Teachers play an intricate role in facilitating connections between authors, students, and families. I encourage preservice teachers to take the following steps as inservice teachers to ensure students fully benefit from author visits:

1. Teachers connect students with an author or illustrator.
2. Teachers couple reading and writing workshops to explore the author's work; students read a genre and discover how to write in the genre.
3. Students annotate author's texts as readers and writers.

4. Students prepare questions to inquire about the author's published work, writing process, writer's craft, experiences, strategies, or profession.
5. The school displays the author's work prominently.
6. Students welcome the author to the classroom, regardless of whether the author visit is in-person or virtual.
7. Recommended: Author models writing and students imitate the modeling in their own writer's notebooks to support transfer of learning.
8. Students write reflections on the author's visit.
9. Students write thank you notes to the author.

Writing festivals and afterschool literacy events connect families with published children's book authors. As one preservice teacher stated in an anonymous course evaluation, "The Young Author's Festival was amazing! It was very insightful to hear from the author herself and the journey through writing her book." Travis stated the following in his eportfolio: "Hearing Toni Buzzeo's speech on specific steps on how she created a book was very fascinating. I learned from her that a lot of time, editing, thought, and trial and error go into creating a published book." Whenever educators connect families with published children's book authors and illustrators, teachers facilitate writing celebrations as Carly stated in her eportfolio:

> The Young Authors' Festival is such an essential resource for the community because it allows educators, children, parents, and current authors and illustrators to come together and celebrate writing.

References

Buzzeo, T. (2003). Author visits made easy. *School Library Journal, 49*(4), 40–41.
Buzzeo, T. (2012). *One cool friend*. [Illustrated by D. Small]. Dial Books.
Crilley, M. (2001–2009). *Akiko* [Series]. Delacorte Books for Young Readers.
Crilley, M. (2007–2008). *Miki Falls* [Series]. HarperCollins Publishers.
Crilley, M. (2010–2016). *Brody's ghost* [Series]. Dark Horse Books.
Curtis, C.P. (1996). *The Watsons go to Birmingham—1963*. Yearling.
Curtis, C.P. (1999). *Bud, not Buddy*. Yearling.
DeFauw, D.L. (2018). One school's yearlong collaboration with a children's book author. *The Reading Teacher, 72*(3), 355–367. doi:10.1002/trtr.1726
DeFauw, D.L., Kriigel, B., & Samet, R. (2017). The University of Michigan–Dearborn's annual young authors' festival. *Michigan Reading Journal, 50*(1), 35–40.
DeFauw, D.L., Kriigel, B., & Samet, R. (2018, March 18). *Ready, set, motivate! Connect students with published children's book authors*. Michigan Reading Association 62nd Annual Conference, Detroit, MI.
Ellis, D. (2009). *The bread winner*. Groundwood Books.

Elster, J.A. (2013). *The colored car*. Wayne State University Press.
Follos, A. (2004). Making an author's visit your best 'good time'. *Teacher Librarian, 31*(5), 8–11.
Giff, P.R. (2004). *Pictures of Hollis Woods*. Yearling.
González, N., Moll, L., & Amanti, C. (2006). *Funds of knowledge: Theorizing practices in households, communities, and classrooms*. Lawrence Erlbaum. doi:10.4324/9781410613462
Gutman, D. (1997). "Author"izing author visits to schools. *The Education Digest, 63*(2), 63–66.
Hagen, C. (2006). *The night Henry Ford met Santa*. [Illustrated by M. Faulkner]. Sleeping Bear Press.
Hayes, S. (2010). Author visits: The Sky(pe)'s the limit. *Voices From the Middle, 17*(3), 56–58.
Kahn, E. (2008). Celebrating Teen Tech Week™ with an author visit. *Young Adult Library Services, 6*(4), 14–16.
Kettel, R. (1996). Reflections on *The Devil's Arithmetic* by a Holocaust survivor: An interview with Jack Wayne—B 8568. *The New Advocate, 9*(4), 287–295.
Lord, C. (2006). *Rules*. Scholastic Press.
Messner, K. (n.d.). Authors who Skype with classes & book clubs (for free!). http://www.katemessner.com/authors-who-skype-with-classes-book-clubs-for-free/
Morgan, H. (2013). Technology in the classroom: Using Skype for exciting projects. *Childhood Education, 89*(3), 197–199. doi:10.1080/00094056.2013.793076
Moynihan, K.E. (2009). Local authors in the classroom: Bringing readers and writers together. *English Journal, 98*(3), 34–38.
Naslund, J., & Jobe, R. (2005). Not just an author visit – It's a literacy event. *School Libraries in Canada, 25*(1), 1–7.
Remenar, K. (2015). *Groundhog's dilemma*. [Illustrated by M. Faulkner]. Charlesbridge.
Schmidt, G.D. (2007). *The Wednesday wars*. Clarion Books.
Silverman, K.N. (2013). Connecting authors to readers through the school library. *Knowledge quest: Rising to the Challenge, 41*(5), 26–29.
Stewart, S. (2012). *The quiet place*. [Illustrated by D. Small]. Farrar Straus Giroux.

6 Evaluate Writing

Discovering Authentic Learning Opportunities through Writing Contests

The Easter Bunny
One night I woke up. Then I went out in the living room. There he was! The Easter Bunny! He was very cute. He had a pink nose. He had long ears. He had a basket in his hands. It had a stuffed rabbit and he had some eggs in it. I didn't say a word. So, he didn't hear me. But I saw what was in the basket.

The Easter Bunny was my first writing contest entry, completed in Mrs. Periat's second-grade classroom. I treasure the classroom anthology that includes our class's responses to the prompt: Write about the Easter Bunny. Other teachers in the building selected the winning entries. For winning first place, Mrs. Periat gave me a stuffed yellow bunny I named Jellybean. The prize is long gone, but not the writing. Most importantly, I have self-identified as a writer since I was in second grade.

I love writing contests. Of the myriad contests I have entered from second grade until now, I have placed in only three: second grade, sixth grade, and as a 40-year-old adult in 2018. I always hope to win, but have experienced little success until the most recent win in 2018 when I was awarded by Michigan's Region of the Society of Children's Book Writers and Illustrators a 2019 mentorship with young adult author Kelly Barson to support my revision process of my middle grade manuscript, *Victory Stumbles*. Of course, winning this contest continues to be a tremendous motivator; however, I continued writing across three decades with minimal writing contest successes. I am not alone.

Children's book authors, Cynthia Leitich Smith and Grace Lin, wrote about their experiences with writing contests. Smith (2017) stated:

> "The Writer's Dream" was the last poem in a collection I wrote during sixth grade ... My goal was to finish in time to enter my school district's competition fair in language arts. Enter I did, though I remember being

disappointed at receiving a white participation ribbon rather than a first-, second-, or third-place award.

(p. 93)

Lin's (2017) personal experience with a writing contest motivated her career choice:

> In my novel *The Year of the Dog*, the main character, Pacy, writes and illustrates a book and sends it to a national book contest. She wins fourth place and $400; and that win cements her dream of becoming an author and illustrator. This is a mostly true story (in fact, the whole novel is 97 percent true). In middle school, I really did enter a national book contest and I did win fourth place.
>
> (p. 155)

Young adult novelists Mildred D. Taylor and Sharon Draper began their writing careers as first-place writing contest winners. Taylor entered the Council on Interracial Books for Children's (CIBC) annual writing contest that began in 1969. The CIBC published 21 winning manuscripts by Native American, Asian American, and African American first-time authors across the next 5 years (Yokota, 2011). Taylor won the contest in 1974 with her first novel, *Song of the Trees*, the first book in her ten-book series of the Logan family. Two years later she won the Newbery Medal for *Roll of Thunder, Hear My Cry*. Draper shared at the 2014 Michigan Reading Association's Conference that she wrote her first book after a ninth-grade student challenged her to write just as she encouraged him to complete his writing homework. She took his challenge, revised, submitted a piece to *Ebony Magazine*'s writing contest, and won first place.

> That really blew me away. But it gave me the affirmation I needed, and the courage to continue, so I wrote a novel. I sent it to 25 publishing companies, got 24 rejections, and one yes. But that was from Simon and Schuster. The book came out, ended up being successful, and they asked me to write a sequel. I have been very blessed and have been privileged to write many more. The writing contest was the catalyst. Life leads us down many pathways. Follow your own path and your own dream. It's a wonderful journey!
>
> (S. Draper, personal communication, September 9, 2018)

My writing journey mirrors Draper's just a bit. A participant in this research study, Roberta, sent me the link to the Michigan's Region of the Society of Children's Book Writers and Illustrators mentorship contest and encouraged me to submit my middle-grade novel. I will always be thankful I took Roberta's advice.

In this chapter, I will detail how writing contests provide an authentic learning opportunity for students since many writers find writing contests motivating. Steps for implementing a writing contest and suggestions for writing contests students may choose to enter are provided. Next, I detail steps to facilitate preservice teachers' authentic evaluation of writing contest entries. Finally, I will detail how to use writing contests for instructional purposes as mentor texts and for standardized assessment preparation. Writing contests are the closest authentic writing opportunity to resemble high-stakes writing assessments: students respond to a prompt for an unknown audience for an evaluative purpose.

Authentic Learning Opportunities through Writing Contests

Writing contests include inherent benefits regardless of whether or not writers win. As noted above, writing contests may provide potential for prosperity as Draper's, Lin's, and Taylor's experiences demonstrate. Writing contests may encourage participation, practice, and promise as Smith's experience illustrates. Writing contests are authentic literacy activities for expert to novice writers, rich with authentic learning potential from publication to standardized assessment preparation for outside-of- and inside-of-school contexts. Writing contests are authentic texts with authentic purposes (Duke et al., 2006).

The benefits of writing contests include: (a) extrinsic motivation as writers are motivated to compete for publication or prizes; (b) high-quality practice as writers commit to the writing process and create an end product; (c) voice development as writers use writer's craft to create high-quality writing selections (Kixmiller, 2004); (d) audience engagement as writers hope to impress their unknown, but real audience (Duke et al., 2006); (e) mentor texts as teachers and students may emulate winning contest entries (DeFauw, 2013, 2015); (f) learning opportunities that bridge home/school connections; and (g) playful writing as writers practice writing in hopes of winning a writing contest. Dewey (1910/1991) stated, "To be playful and serious at the same time is possible, and it defines the ideal mental condition" (p. 218). Even while *playing*, writers understand the highest-quality writing will be rewarded through the writing contest and submit their best work.

Numerous writing contests are available for writers of all ages. For elementary students, I detail 24 writing contest opportunities in two previous publications (DeFauw, 2013, 2015). A quick Google search for "writing contests for kids" yields 33,600,000 hits. Writing contests motivate many writers, just like the following four participants' quotes highlight:

The one great memory I have of writing happened in about second or third grade. They had a writing competition where every student wrote their own story and the winner was chosen from each class. The best part was that each winning story was brought to life by a group of actors and performed in front of the whole school. To my surprise, my story was the class winner. It was probably one of the greatest moments of my young life because nothing special like that had ever happened to me. When it was my story's time to be performed, they sat me in a director's chair at the front of the gym so I could have the first view of my story. I had never felt so special, and it is something I will never forget.

(Amber, Writing History Essay, Fall 2019)

Another memory of writing as a child that I have includes the time I won a writing contest in my fifth-grade class. I remember it was called something along the lines of the "Brainstormers." It was a fictional story that I vaguely remember being about a bear as one of the main characters. Each student in every grade submitted a paper and the winners' stories were read in front of the entire school.

(Paula, Writing History Essay, Fall 2018)

I would say a positive writing experience I had was when I was in … 8th grade. We had to write an essay … about an American Hero to me. I wrote about my grandma. She was recently diagnosed with Cancer that year and she like basically raised me and my brother and sister so it was really special to me to write about her. And I think it was a contest. I didn't win but it was in the top three of my school so I was really proud of it.

(Harper, Post-Course Interview, February 12, 2015)

I remember … like third or fourth grade, maybe second grade … my teacher came to me and recommended that I enter an entry into some sort of writing contest. And I remember just like being really happy, like really proud of myself … because I don't think she, as far as I know, she didn't ask anyone else in class. So, I felt like I was like, special or something. And I mean, the piece I turned out was pretty bad, to be honest … but I remember that there was a word limit. And I went past it in my initial piece and I didn't cut it down. I just said like TO BE CONTINUED like that was going to be fine. But that's not how it works. So, it was just a really bad piece overall, but I was really happy that I got chosen out of everyone to like, enter that contest. So that's one positive experience.

(Ryder, Post-Course Interview, February 9, 2017)

And although not a contest per se, I argue writing scholarship essays and writing for publication are contest-like experiences. Travis stated the following:

> A positive [experience] is writing ... a scholarship ... several years back I wrote a few ... different pieces of writing that I submitted and one of them came back and they said they liked my writing I submitted and I was awarded a lot of money for my writing.
>
> (Travis, Post-Course Interview, February 9, 2015)

Writing contests include potential drawbacks for most students since few writers win. Writing contests could demoralize, demotivate, or deject some writers. Yet no participants mentioned writing contests as a negative experience. Many writers find writing contests motivating. For third- through fifth-grade students, the YAF committee implements a writing contest.

Implementing a Writing Contest

The third- through fifth-grade writing contest is hosted each September and October through the YAF. Students write an essay, narrative, or poem per the YAF's theme which the YAF committee determines after reading the guest author and/or illustrator's book(s). Contest details are available at http://library.umd.umich.edu/yaf/writingcontest.php. About 30 schools have participated in the writing contest with 150 to 250 entries submitted annually for the last seven years. Ultimately, writing contests are easy to implement per the following steps:

1. Select the grade-level range.
2. Determine genres.
3. Craft a set of writing prompts with suggestions for writers to choose.
4. Determine how and by whom writing contests will be evaluated. Post the rubric.
5. Award writers for participation and/or placing in the writing contest.

The writing contest provides our preservice teachers enrolled in the flipped writing methodology course with an authentic assessment opportunity for grading elementary students' writing. The evaluation process extends across two to four of our in-person sessions, depending on the number of entries and preservice teachers' preparation for evaluating writing contests reliably. Presently, preservice teachers use the National Assessment Governing Board (2017) preliminary holistic scoring guides for persuasion, explanation, or real/imagined experience (pp. 59–70).

To prepare for the evaluation process, preservice teachers complete an assessment module. In-person, preservice teachers are provided with an anthology published the previous year so they can use the past winning entries as anchor sets. Each anthology includes ten entries: first, second, and third place for third, fourth, and fifth grades plus a grand-prize winner. Using the holistic rubric, I model how to evaluate the grand-prize and the first-place writing content entries for each grade level, conducting a think aloud as I determine the holistic score for a fifth-grade, fourth-grade, and third-grade piece. I model scoring the grand-prize and first-place entries to show preservice teachers few writing contest entries earn the rubrics' highest scores of 6. Preservice teachers record the four scores I determine on the anthology, a step they continue throughout the in-person sessions to create an anchor set of scored entries to use as reference for grading the current year's writing contest entries.

To continue the preparation for the evaluation process, I model the small-group evaluation process with two volunteers. Three of us sit in a circle in front of the class to model how each of us: (a) chooses one of the second-place entries for each grade level; (b) reads the entry; and (c) determines a holistic score. The scores are written on a sticky note and then folded in half to keep the scores secret before sharing the writing contest entry with the reader to our right. The second reader evaluates the same entry we read and writes a score on top of the folded sticky note. The second reader compares their score to the previous reader's score. If the scores are exact, the second reader circles the score written on top of the sticky note. If the first and second readers' scores are one number apart, a half score is determined. For example, if reader one gives the writing selection a 4 and reader two gives the writing selection a 3, the second reader writes and circles a final score of 3.5 on the sticky note. If the first and second readers' scores are more than one point apart another sticky note is placed on top of the folded sticky note. The third reader reads the entry without knowing the previous two scores. If the third reader's score matches the first or second reader's scores, that is the determined score. If the third reader's score is one point apart from the first or second reader's scores, a half score is determined. If the scores do not match, the average of the three readers' scores may be used as the final score (Johnson et al., 2000), but on the rare instances when this happens, usually with poetry, I evaluate the writing contest entry to determine a score.

To complete the preparation process before identifying the winning contest entries for the current year, in groups of three, students practice the same process with the third-place winning entries detailed in the anthology. Then, each group receives a grade-level portion of the entries, uses the holistic writing rubrics, refers to the anchor set created in the anthology, and follows the same method modeled for scoring the writing contest.

Finally, I analyze the scoring results and identify each grade level's top submissions, usually five or six entries per grade level. I read aloud the top entries and preservice teachers vote on the top four entries for each grade level to determine the first-, second-, and third-place winning contest entries. Then, preservice teachers determine which first-place entry earns the grand prize. For whichever grade level wins the grand-prize, the fourth-place entry moves up to third place and bumps up each of the two higher entries one level. Preservice teachers find this experience valuable as Harper and Celeste shared:

> It was such an honor and learning experience to assess the writing for the 2014 Young Authors' Festival and decide who the winning authors would be ... It gave me some insight to how difficult it is to assess writing, and how beneficial it is to do it as a teaching team.
> (Harper, EPortfolio, Fall 2014)

> I've never actually graded writing, so being able to do that was really cool, and I thought that was really helpful too to be working with your peers because I mean future teaching, one day, if you're grading something and you're kind of unsure, you could always refer back to a colleague or ask a peer for help with it.
> (Celeste, Post-Course Interview, February 19, 2019)

Determining the grand-prize winner often creates animated conversation as the scores for the first-place winners are often so close the preservice teachers must choose the grand-prize winner. Hannah stated:

> I like the process, because I've never really ... evaluated students' work before. And so, when we did it, at first, it was kind of hard to choose which number to give them, because I don't have much background knowledge of what the certain grade should be at in terms of writing. It was fun to do it. But once you got down to like, between two papers, which one should be number one, that's when it got hard because you have the other classmates who pick this one writing and then you're picking B and you're trying to see what they see and what made them pick that writing and not the other.
> (Hannah, Post-Course Interview, May 8, 2018)

At the YAF, although all writing contest participants are encouraged to attend, the first-, second-, and third-place winners from each grade level plus the grand-prize winner are encouraged to read aloud their winning writing contest entries to the YAF audience, a feat Megan found inspiring:

> I think it's amazing that all of those students were brave enough to say or speak in front of everybody. And their writing was phenomenal. And so, when I think about that, it makes me want to be the best writing teacher I can be, because I would like to see my future students standing up there. (Megan, Post-Course Interview, October 10, 2019)

The winners receive Barnes and Noble gift cards: $100 for the grand prize, $75 for first place, $50 for second place, and $25 for third place. In 2014, the fourth-grade first-place winner submitted her entry to another local writing contest and won the grand prize in 2015. Certainly, that student felt motivated to participate in writing contests.

An anthology of the winning contest entries is given to each child. We recommend attendees use the anthology as mentor texts (DeFauw, 2013, 2015), which writers and teachers may use to support students' writing development. I also encourage preservice teachers to use writing contests to support high-stakes standardized writing assessment preparation.

Preparation for High-Stakes Standardized Writing Assessments

Most educators agree standardized writing assessments are inauthentic, yet many teachers must provide students mock, on-demand prompts to prepare students for high-stakes standardized writing assessments to meet state and district requirements (Olinghouse et al., 2012). Even though Hillocks' (2002) seminal study detailed the negative impact high-stakes writing assessments create for classroom instruction and curricular content, "teach to the test" remains a reality in too many classrooms as standardized writing assessments continue to impact writing curricula (Au & Gourd, 2013; Bhattacharyya et al., 2013; O'Neill et al., 2005). For example, in the Michigan Student Test of Education Progress (M-STEP), students complete on-demand writing prompts where they synthesize evidence from two sources (Hindman, 2015). To help teachers prepare students for the MSTEP, the Michigan Association of Intermediate School Administrators (MAISA) advise teachers to use Calkins' (2015) performance assessments that incorporate on-demand contexts for narratives, informational/explanatory, and argument genres.

Regardless of whether or not we agree with on-demand, high-stakes writing assessments, most states in the United States require students to perform satisfactorily on prompted standardized writing assessments; thus, teachers teach students and provide time to experience success in such assessment contexts

(Angelillo, 2005). If we already have to prepare students using such writing instruction as on-demand prompts for standardized writing assessment preparation, then I argue we are obligated to make the preparation as authentic as possible. Kixmiller (2004) stated, "A classroom that includes authentic writing is student-centered, interest-based, and meaning-driven instead of assessment centered, score-based, and accountability driven" (p. 30).

One way to make high-stakes standardized writing assessment instruction more authentic is to require students to respond to authentic writing contest prompts, since writing contests are the closest authentic writing opportunity to resemble high-stakes writing assessments (DeFauw, 2015). In both contexts, students respond to a prompt for an unknown audience for evaluative purposes. In both contexts, students are unlikely to receive feedback. Students are often motivated to write contest entries well in hopes of winning the contest (Jocson et al., 2006).

Writing in response to writing contest prompts will not scaffold student learning (Gallimore & Tharp, 1990). If students view writing contests or the repetitive use of writing contests as boring, the implementation of the strategy may actually decrease writing (Zimmerman & Schunk, 2008) and create disinterest in writing, which could be detrimental to students' writing development. Bruner (1966) stated, "External reinforcement may indeed get a particular act going and may even lead to its repetition, but it does not nourish, reliably, the long course of learning" (p. 128). Especially with writing contests, students must see the potential reward of winning a writing contest as valuable in order for writing contests to support their motivation for writing. Jocson et al. (2006) conducted a participatory ethnographic study in which they studied the effects of contest writing on high school students. Ninth- and tenth-grade students found purpose in submitting their poetry to the June Jordan Poetry Prize Contest.

A writing contest prompt may inspire a student to write and play a competitive game; thus, teachers may use writing contests to spark students' interest in writing (Jocson et al., 2006). "Situational interest can be effectively utilized to promote academic motivation ... and help [students] make cognitive gains in areas that initially hold little interest for them" (Hidi & Harackiewicz, 2000, p. 156). Writing contests may create situational interest as writing contests trigger students' interest and create a learning context in which students want to impress an evaluative audience to win prizes. Teachers may use this trigger to invite students into the writing process and then maintain their interest (Hidi & Renninger, 2006).

Using Writing Contest Entries as Mentor Texts

Writing contests also provide mentor texts. As a former third-grade teacher, using winning contest entries as mentor texts motivated my students. My students felt they could write like the students who won the writing contests because those entries, written by authors their own age, seemed like writing "they themselves could produce, [and so they would] write vicariously with the authors" (Smith, 1983, p. 565). Additionally, students' suggestions for how the contest winner should have revised created teachable moments regarding writer's craft.

Although the YAF committee does not publish online the anthology of winning contest entries, many organizations that host writing clinics publish past entries, such as The Writing Conference, Inc. (http://writingconference.com/wpwritingconference/), The Grannie Annie Family Story Celebration (http://thegrannieannie.org/), and Creative Communications: A Celebration of Today's Writers (https://poeticpower.com/).

I encourage preservice teachers to use writing contest entries as mentor texts with their future students in and outside of school. Interestingly, this study's data does not reflect a single instance of preservice teachers using winning contests as mentor texts, even though the writing clinic follows the YAF. Moving forward, I need to revise some lessons to include writing contests as mentor texts. I also encourage preservice teachers to understand how writing contests may facilitate home/school connections. The more writing contests students participate in, the more they practice writing for an authentic purpose and audience.

References

Angelillo, J. (2005). *Writing to the prompt: When students don't have a choice.* Heinemann.

Au, W., & Gourd, K. (2013). Asinine assessment: Why high-stakes testing is bad for everyone, including English teachers. *English Journal, 103*(1), 14–19.

Bhattacharyya, S., Junot, M., & Clark, H. (2013). Can you hear us? Voices raised against standardized testing by novice teachers. *Creative Education, 4*(10), 633–639. doi:10.4236/ce.2013.410091

Bruner, S. (1966). *Toward a theory of instruction.* The Belknap Press of Harvard University Press.

Calkins, L. (2015). *Writing pathways: Performance assessment learning progressions, grades K–8.* Heinemann.

Carey, K. (2015). *MAISA.* gomaisa-public.rubiconatlas.org

DeFauw, D.L. (2013). 10 writing opportunities to 'teach to the test'. *The Reading Teacher, 66*(7), 569–573. doi:10.1002/TRTR.1161

DeFauw, D.L. (2015). Using authentic writing contests to prepare third graders for high stakes standardized assessments. *Language Arts Journal of Michigan, 31*(1), 9–19. doi:10.9707/2168-149X.2091

Dewey, J. (1910/1991). *How we think.* Prometheus Books. doi:10.1037/10903-000

Duke, N.K., Purcell-Gates, V., Hall, L.A., & Tower, C. (2006). Authentic literacy activities for developing comprehension and writing. *The Reading Teacher, 60*(4), 344–355. doi:10.1598/RT.60.4.4

Gallimore, R., & Tharp, R. (1990). Teaching mind in society: Teaching, schooling, and literate discourse. In L.C. Moll (Ed.), *Vygotsky and education: Instructional* implications and applications of sociohistorical psychology (pp. 175–205). Cambridge University Press. doi:10.1017/CBO9781139173674

Hidi, S., & Harackiewicz, J.M. (2000). Motivating the academically unmotivated: A critical issue for the 21st century. *Review of Educational Research, 70*(2), 151–179. doi:10.3102/00346543070002151

Hidi, S., & Renninger, K.A. (2006). The four-phase model of interest development. *Educational Psychologist, 41*(2), 111–127. doi:10.1207/s15326985ep4102_4

Hillocks, G., Jr. (2002). *The testing trap: How state writing assessments control learning.* Teachers College Press.

Hindman, S. (2015). English Language Arts M-STEP. *Michigan Reading Journal, 47*(2), 54–55.

Jocson, K., Burnside, S., & Collins, M. (2006). Pens on the prize: Linking school and community through contest inspired literacy. *Multicultural Education, 14*(2), 28–33.

Johnson, R.L., Penny, J., & Gordon, B. (2000). The relation between score resolution methods and interrater reliability: An empirical study of an analytic scoring rubric. *Applied Measurement in Education, 13*(2), 121–138. doi:10.1207/S15324818AME1302_1

Kixmiller, L.A.S. (2004). Standards without sacrifice: The case for authentic writing. *English Journal, 94*(1), 29–33. doi:10.2307/4128844

Lin, G. (2017). Grace Lin. In E.B. Weissman (Ed.), *Our story begins: Your favorite authors and illustrators share fun, inspiring, and occasionally ridiculous things they wrote and drew as kids* (pp. 155–167). Atheneum Books for Young Readers.

National Assessment Governing Board. (2017). *Writing framework for the 2017 National Assessment Educational Progress.* U.S. Department of Education. https://www.nagb.gov/content/nagb/assets/documents/publications/frameworks/writing/2017-writing-framework.pdf

O'Neill, P., Murphy, S., Huot, B., & Williamson, M.M. (2005). What teachers say about different kinds of mandated state writing tests. *Journal of Writing Assessment, 2*(2), 81–108.

Olinghouse, N.G., Zheng, J., & Morlock, L. (2012). State writing assessment: Inclusion of motivational factors in writing tasks. *Reading & Writing Quarterly: Overcoming Learning Difficulties, 28*(1), 97–119. doi:10.1080/10573569.2012.632736

Smith, C.L. (2017). Cynthia Leitich Smith. In E.B. Weissman (Ed.), *Our story begins: Your favorite authors and illustrators share fun, inspiring, and occasionally ridiculous things they wrote and drew as kids* (pp. 155–167). Atheneum Books for Young Readers.

Smith, F. (1983). Reading like a writer. *Language Arts, 60*(5), 558–567.

Taylor, M.D. (1974). *Song of the trees.* Dial Press.

Taylor, M.D. (1976). *Roll of thunder, hear my cry.* Dial Press.

Yokota, J. (2011). Awards in literature for children and adolescents. In S.A. Wolf, K. Coats, P. Enciso, & C.A. Jenkins (Eds.), *Handbook of research on children's and young adult literature* (pp. 467–478). Routledge.

Zimmerman, B.J., & Schunk, D.H. (2008). Motivation: An essential dimension of self-regulated learning. In D.H. Schunk & B.J. Zimmerman (Eds.), *Motivation and self-regulated learning: Theory, research, and applications* (pp. 1–30). Lawrence Erlbaum Associates.

Part III

Transferring Pedagogical Content Knowledge of Writing to Future Classrooms

7 Transfer Flipped Learning Opportunities
Building Home/School Connections Virtually

Although the flipped writing methodology course focuses on pedagogical content knowledge of writing (PCKW) as preservice teachers use flipped learning components as learners, I also aim for preservice teachers to create flipped learning opportunities as educators for (a) their future students, and (b) the families who attend the Young Authors' Festival (YAF) or peruse the YAF's parent resource page available at http://guides.umd.umich.edu/yafparents. I will detail in this chapter how I teach preservice teachers to use flipped learning technology to benefit students and their families. First, I will explore how technology connects to PCKW. Next, I will detail how preservice teachers create flipped learning family resources. Finally, I will address the following research questions:

1. How will preservice teachers apply PCKW through ASL projects (e.g., third-grade writing clinic and YAF)?
2. How will preservice teachers transfer their learning from their flipped writing methodology course to their future teaching experiences as preservice and inservice teachers?

Technological Pedagogical and Content Knowledge (TPACK)

To use flipped learning as educators, preservice teachers must develop their technological pedagogical (and) content knowledge (TPCK) (Mishra & Koehler, 2006). Thompson and Mishra (2007–2008) renamed the acronym TPCK to support pronunciation and portray the interconnectedness between the three components.

> TPACK is the basis of effective teaching with technology, requiring an understanding of the representation of concepts using technologies; pedagogical techniques that use technologies in constructive ways to teach

content; knowledge of what makes concepts difficult or easy to learn and how technology can help redress some of the problems that students face; knowledge of students' prior knowledge and theories of epistemology; and knowledge of how technologies can be used to build on existing knowledge to develop new epistemologies or strengthen old ones.

(Koehler & Mishra, 2009, p. 66)

Mishra (2019) changed the TPACK diagram to enclose the three overlapping circles of technological knowledge, pedagogical knowledge, and content knowledge within contextual knowledge. (If the diagram is new to you, I invite you to conduct a quick Google search for TPACK.) Similarly, Shulman and Shulman (2004) extended Shulman's (1986, 1987) notion of pedagogical content knowledge to evolve from an individualistic to "a more comprehensive conception of teacher learning and development within communities and contexts" (Shulman & Shulman, 2004, p. 259). Teachers' knowledge of their teaching context is paramount to understanding how teachers utilize TPACK to facilitate student learning.

Angeli and Valanides (2009) argued a strand of TPACK or TPCK is information and communication technology (ICT); ICT-TPCK conceptualizes the knowledge teachers demonstrate as they create and utilize technology in conjunction with their pedagogical content knowledge to facilitate student learning.

> The ways knowledge about tools and their pedagogical affordances, pedagogy, content, learners, and context are synthesized into an understanding of how particular topics that are difficult to be understood by learners, or difficult to be represented by teachers, can be transformed and taught more effectively with ICT.
>
> (Angeli & Valanides, 2009, pp. 158–159)

To facilitate the preservice teachers' ICT use, I (a) model how to use technology, (b) use instructional design to facilitate the authentic flipped learning family resources' creation made available through the YAF parent webpage, (c) encourage collaboration during two in-person sessions to practice the screencast technology, and (d) provide feedback (Tondeur et al., 2012). Preservice teachers need to practice creating flipped learning resources to facilitate their self-efficacy in utilizing flipped learning as inservice teachers.

Using flipped learning components available through the Google Suite, such as screencasts, Google folders, Google docs, video links, and other online resources, preservice teachers create flipped learning family resources similarly to how I create course modules. Although I stress student-centered instruction throughout course content, the technology in both contexts (modules and flipped learning family resources) is used to create more teacher-centered instruction. Hussey et al. (2014) argued it is easier for faculty to flip teacher-centered lecture content. Teacher-centered, module content is more active because preservice teachers can access content as often as needed to support their individualized learning needs (Foertsch et al., 2002). Similar to the in-person course and online module designs, preservice teachers create the in-person parent session for the YAF, which they flip for the flipped learning family resource assignment with hope the YAF committee will choose their flipped resource to post to the YAF parent webpage.

Flipping a Family Resource

To support preservice teachers' TPACK development, I provide the transparently designed assignment (Winkelmes et al., 2016): flipped learning family resource. Winkelmes et al. (2016) discovered transparently designed assignments provide an effective instructional intervention to support underserved students' achievement. The assignment description specifies the assignment's purpose, skill development, knowledge, helpful resources, sequenced tasks, and criteria outlined on a detailed rubric. The assignment's purpose follows:

> Educators know how important it is to collaborate with families. So often, families want to support their children's schooling, but do not know what to do. As educators, we can support students' learning, even more, when we empower their families with strategies they can use at home to support the home/school connection. The purpose of this task is to provide you an opportunity to reflect on families' needs and design a resource to connect home and school.

Through the assignment, preservice teachers practice the following essential skills:

- Collaborate with others and consider how empowering families may support your students.
- Create materials to support student learning.
- Reflect on your teaching.
- Understand families are vested stakeholders.
- Embrace families as allies.

Preservice teachers have minimal, if any, experience developing content to support families, especially through flipped learning. Using the Google Suite, I teach preservice teachers to create flipped learning family resources across the semester following the steps detailed in Chapter 2. The steps encompass the sequenced tasks and helpful resources required for successful completion of the flipped learning family resource.

Step One: Determine the Content You Need to Teach

Through a required module, I help preservice teachers determine parent-session topics they will first implement in-person at the YAF and then virtually through the flipped learning family resource. I refer preservice teachers to the International Literacy Association and the National Council of Teachers of English website http://readwritethink.org/ for mentor texts of parent resources. We navigate to the Parent & Afterschool Resources webpage, scroll to the Tips & How-To's section and use the Tips for Teaching Writing resources where each tip provides an explanation of why the writing tip is beneficial with step-by-step directions for implementation. We review an example such as Help a Child Write a Story, focusing on the action steps families may use at home. Additionally, I share examples of support the DeFauw family may need and invite preservice teachers to ask parents about resources they need. I also provide an example of a step-by-step, fifteen-minute, parent-session guide preservice teachers may use as a mentor text to prepare for the YAF. The guide sheet includes the following action steps I would use in-person with parent-writers as detailed in DeFauw (2017), an article I require preservice teachers to read:

1. Summarize *Sky Color* by Peter H. Reynolds, published by Scholastic, showing families the cover and flipping through the pages.
2. Identify the writing task for the book: create a list of colors. Ask families: "Have you ever talked with your child about what colors mean to you?"
3. Read aloud an excerpt from the picture book to the families.
4. Model for families how to respond to the writing task in a one-minute freewrite, creating your own list of colors you loved as a child or enjoy as an adult.
5. Invite families to complete a similar freewrite in response to the reading excerpt and writing task. Encourage families to write to the prompt for two to three minutes.
6. Continue to write as the families write, perhaps adding to the modeled writing.
7. Invite volunteers to share their writing with a partner and then volunteers share whole group. Potentially share the added details included in the modeled writing to increase families' participation.
8. Encourage families to share their writing with their children.

Transfer Flipped Learning Opportunities 109

9. Challenge families to write at home with their children in response to materials they read aloud.
10. Send families home with the handout that includes other picture book titles and writing prompt suggestions.

Step Two: Choose to Use Flipped Writing Pedagogies

Although preservice teachers do not independently choose to use flipped learning pedagogies since they are required to flip the in-person YAF parent-session content, the flipped learning family resource assignment is designed to empower them to choose to use flipped learning as inservice teachers. To prepare preservice teachers for this assignment, during the two in-person sessions following the YAF, I teach preservice teachers about flipped learning pedagogy. I define flipped learning, provide examples, and highlight how I utilize flipped learning specifically to teach them the PCKW they apply throughout the course's academic service learning projects. This flipped learning lecture is the only lecture I provide in-person as I model for preservice teachers how to use screencast technology and organize materials in a Google folder.

Step Three: Select Content to Deliver through Flipped Writing Pedagogies

Preservice teachers identify the content from their YAF parent session that they will deliver through flipped learning pedagogies. I model this process using the guide sheet I provide as a mentor text, especially since some steps for the in-person session are not conducive to flipped learning contexts. The following is an example of how I transfer the action steps I would take with parent-writers to a flipped learning family resource through a screencast, unless noted otherwise:

1. Summarize *Sky Color* by Peter H. Reynolds, published by Scholastic, showing a cover of the book from the author's website. Encourage families to borrow the book from their local library to read aloud together.
2. Share with families the writing task you recommend they connect to this picture book: create a list of colors. Encourage families to reflect for a moment: "Have you ever talked with your child about what colors mean to you?"
3. Use a Google doc to model for families how to respond to the writing task in a one-minute freewrite, creating your own list of colors you loved as a child, or enjoy as an adult.

4. Invite families to pause the screencast and complete a similar freewrite to the prompt for two to three minutes, as modeled.
5. Encourage families to share their writing with their children.
6. Challenge families to write at home with their children in response to the materials they read aloud.
7. Refer families to the Google folder that includes an electronic handout with other picture book titles and writing prompt suggestions.

The flipped learning family resource is shared as a link to the Google folder. Within the Google folder is a Google doc with a link to the screencast, the Google doc used to model the freewrite, and an electronic copy of the handout with additional picture book suggestions.

Although preservice teachers implement the YAF parent session in partnerships, they create their flipped learning family resource independently. Partnerships are allotted time in class to co-plan content delivery through technology. For example, partners determine the content they need to flip such as the presentation they need to record through a screencast and the handout they provide families. If preservice teachers model a strategy, they also need to consider how they will demonstrate such modeling through the flipped learning family resource. Requiring preservice teachers to create the flipped learning family resource independently ensures each preservice teacher practices flipped learning components fully; thus, increasing the likelihood they will choose to use flipped learning as inservice teachers.

Step Four: Determine the Resources You have Available to Flip Course Content

Preservice teachers learn about available resources to flip the content from their in-person YAF parent session to a virtual family resource. During the session following the YAF, I highlight the Google Suite resources and walk preservice teachers through Chapter 2's content for Step Four. Preservice teachers download Screencastify, practice using a Google folder for hyperlinked resources, and create a screencast during class with their partners (for practice).

Step Five: Flip Course Content to Facilitate Flipped Learning

Outside of class, preservice teachers create their flipped learning family resource independently using screencast software. I used to recommend preservice teachers use Screencastify's free, 10-minute version, but recently the limit changed to 5 minutes. Within a Google folder, preservice teachers link to handouts and a succinct screencast, no more than 10 minutes.

Screencasts and other resources available from the Google Suite are simpler forms of ICT in comparison to other software available. Professionally, I need support with many software programs available to teachers. Certainly, technology can integrate ICT-TPACK in higher-quality ways than I currently teach preservice teachers enrolled in the course. For example, Angeli and Valanides (2005) studied preservice teachers' software use to provide science instruction through three phases. Admittedly, preservice teachers enrolled in this flipped writing methodology course demonstrate what preservice teachers in phase one of Angeli and Valanides (2005) demonstrated:

> [P]reservice teachers in phases one and two did not use the ICT tools to support learner-centered teaching strategies or integrate the tools with appropriate pedagogy in the classroom, but they only used the tools to support existing old teaching practices. In contrast, participants in phase three exhibited a statistically significant greater technology competency in using ICT to support iterative teaching strategies and integrate them with appropriate inquiry-based pedagogy in classroom instruction. These results indicate that the aspects of ICT-related [Pedagogical Content Knowledge] concerning use of ICT to support teaching strategies and integration of ICT activities with appropriate pedagogy in the classroom may be the most difficult to develop, and that some ICT tools have the technological affordances to guide the design of more constructivist learning activities.
>
> (p. 300)

Impact of Flipped Learning Family Resources on Preservice Teachers' Transfer of Learning

The research study theme, transferring as evidence and vision, is evident in data collected in Fall 2018 from Celeste, Jacob, Megan, Paula, and Renee; and in Fall 2019 from Amber, Jackie, Maceo, and Sana. The YAF committee reviews all flipped learning family resources and selects a few each semester to post to our parent resource page available at http://guides.umd.umich.edu/yafparents. To keep the participants' identity confidential, I will address the participants' transfer of learning generally as participants' flipped learning family resources may or may not be posted to the webpage. Participants explored the following topics addressed throughout the course:

- Freewriting,
- Modeling,
- Promoting conversation through dialogue journals and read aloud conversations,

- Using sentence variety and sentence stems, and
- Writing authority lists.

Some participants explored the following topics not addressed through course content:

- Art and crafts,
- Literary devices, and
- Playing word games.

Although one preservice teacher provided no screencast (reason unknown) and another preservice teacher provided a video of them teaching the content just as they taught at the YAF (due to a lack of technology access), all other participants showcased their teacher presence within screencasts. In each screencast, preservice teachers provided tips and tricks for families to consider using at home to support home/school connections. Preservice teachers explored subjects across content areas, using flipped learning to support families in subjects such as reading, writing, and math. Many preservice teachers encouraged word play and conversation. Despite the use of a transparently designed assignment (Winkelmes et al., 2016), some preservice teachers included only a screencast with no additional resources, which impacted their rubric score. Without practice, preservice teachers would not be empowered to use flipped learning technology.

Preservice teachers seemed to take-for-granted the course design with flipped learning as evident in the interview data. In the interviews from Fall 2014 and Fall 2016, preservice teachers did not mention flipped learning. Without specific practice with flipped learning technologies, preservice teachers did not demonstrate transfer nor a vision to use flipped learning in their own classrooms. Beginning with Fall 2017 interviews, I specifically asked preservice teachers to share their perceptions regarding the flipped learning components inherent in the course design, but Fall 2017 participants only mentioned Canvas modules.

In the Fall 2018 and 2019 interviews, preservice teachers did not mention flipped learning until I asked them to discuss their experiences with flipped learning. Jackie summed up how many preservice teachers seem to view flipped learning:

> Flipped learning is notetaking in my mind. It's like notetaking outside of the classroom, like kind of on your own time, which is nice. I like that a lot. I like going at my own pace with flipped learning and it's nice being able to choose what environment I'm in for when I'm notetaking. It also makes class more enjoyable because we're never notetaking in class.
> (Jackie, Post-Course Interview, January 22, 2020)

Because Fall 2018 and 2019 preservice teachers completed the flipped learning family resource assignment, they seemed prepared to respond regarding how they may or may not use flipped learning as inservice teachers. Additionally, some preservice teachers completed the technology in education course prior to taking the flipped writing methodology course, as evident in Celeste's quote:

> I like flipped learning. I remember one of my technology classes we did a flipped classroom where we did a lesson online so we had a bunch of links … to different videos and resources and then at the end of all that there would be like a questionnaire like a handout worksheet to make sure they actually followed through with everything and went through it. I think it's a good resource to do the flipped classroom but at the same time it could be kind of tough depending on where you're working because if your students don't have access to electronics or to computers at home then it's kind of tough for them to take part in the flipped classroom.
> (Celeste, Post-Course Interview, February 19, 2019)

Addressing students' technology access is imperative. If Celeste or other preservice teachers discover their students do not have access to technology, as we discuss in class, teachers must provide the content differently such as providing technology access before, during, or after school; downloading content to other devices or files students can access at home; or providing hard copies as needed. Jacob also addressed teachers knowing their students in order to ensure successful flipped learning implementation:

> I also think it helps with accountability, student accountability when they're learning the material at home. It's essentially up to them at this point. And I think, as a teacher, I'm trying to make my kids independent, and part of that is them being accountable for themselves … I also think that you have to know your kids, because it might work for one group, but it might not work for the next group … Getting to know your kids and building relationships with them is very important. So, you can see if maybe flipped learning would work in your classroom one year, and, you know, try it again next year.
> (Jacob, Post-Course Interview, May 23, 2019)

When teachers are certain their students have access to technology at home, they may provide flipped resources to support writing instruction. Zurcher (2016) shared strategies inservice teachers could implement to combat scarcity of time during the writing workshop. She stressed teachers need to include families in their students' writing instruction in and outside of school. She encouraged teachers to invite parents to school literacy nights to provide suggestions to parents on how they may want to provide their students with writing feedback and create family writing opportunities. Although she did not mention flipping resources, the ideas she highlights would flip easily and ensure access to anyone with technology. Teachers could create a screencast or video of them modeling how they provide constructive feedback, which transfers to at-home experiences. Although flipping resources takes time, creating resources for families empowers them with tools they can use at home. "Any time spent coordinating or communicating with parents will be recovered and multiplied in the future as parents become allies in the writing classroom" (Zurcher, 2016, p. 368).

Reflections Regarding the Flipped Learning Family Resource

Most preservice teachers' flipped learning family resources are 'schoolcentric' and not 'familycentric' strategies (Pushor & Amendt, 2018). I continue to reflect on how to teach preservice teachers to support families, because I think it is problematic for preservice teachers to learn they need to provide families with strategies as the flipped learning family resource assignment portrays. Celeste stated:

> I think to talk more so to parents about the writing because a lot of parents I feel like don't really know the writing process too well and I think it was really helpful for us to give them resources so they could go home and help their kids. And then I also thought it was kind of nice because we did have some parents ask us for stuff so that was kind of cool to hear from them and what they thought was helpful.
> (Celeste, Post-Course Interview, February 19, 2019)

I anticipate most parents are familiar with the writing process and most, if not all, of the topics preservice teachers address through their flipped learning family resources. Preservice teachers need to learn from families. I need to connect preservice teachers to families in mutually beneficial ways to learn from one another versus preservice teachers "teaching" families content.

Pushor and Amendt (2018) encourage school leaders to support teachers' belief development related to working with families. Additionally, InTASC standards require teachers understand family impact on student learning:

> 10(m) The teacher understands that alignment of family, school, and community spheres of influence enhances student learning and that discontinuity in these spheres of influence interferes with learning.
> (Council of Chief State School Officers Interstate Teacher Assessment and Support Consortium, 2013, p. 45)

Through the data, some preservice teachers demonstrate a schoolcentric versus a familycentric stance (Pushor, 2015). Parents are their children's first and longest-standing educators. I question how my own White, middle class values are perpetuated through this assignment even though I want to push myself and the preservice teachers to view home/school literacy opportunities through a familycentric lens. Pushor and Amendt (2018) encourage authentic opportunities to engage families and teachers:

> We discussed how teachers' dispositions are often schoolcentric, reflecting a predominantly middle-class and white mind and character. To interrupt such a disposition, we believe it is important for a school leader to consider the notion of disposition as a verb, as an act. Taken up in this way, such an action becomes lived as a carefully designed and implemented professional development process. The school leader guides teachers to become awake to their current disposition, thus enabling them to consider what is taken-for-granted in their stance and what may require informed rethinking ... and take up a new position, one that shifts a schoolcentric stance to one that is familycentric in nature.
>
> (pp. 7–8)

Although the flipped learning family resource assignment needs revision to align to a familycentric position (Pushor & Amendt, 2018), parents supported the preservice teachers' learning as Jackie's quote highlights:

> I wasn't that nervous honestly to present for the parent resource ... When I saw how many parents actually showed up ... I thought that there was a lot of parents there. And then when they all like crowded around, it got a little nerve wracking ... I didn't really think that they were going to take these parent resources that seriously especially because ... they were getting tickets from them. I kind of thought they were just gonna listen and move along. But a lot of them were taking pictures and asking us questions, and they wanted our handouts. Like they genuinely, I think, found value in what we were teaching. And I was just surprised because I just I didn't think they were going to actually want to use our resource in real life. It's easy to be like, "Oh yeah, maybe I'll use that one day," and kind of like, tell someone, "Oh yeah, this is good." But when you are taking pictures of the posters and asking more questions, I can just tell that they genuinely actually wanted to use our resource.
>
> (Jackie Post-Course Interview, January 22, 2020)

References

Angeli, C., & Valanides, N. (2005). Preservice elementary teachers as information and communication technology designers: An instructional systems design model based on an expanded view of pedagogical content knowledge. *Journal of Computer Assisted Learning, 21*(4), 292–302. doi:10.1111/j.1365-2729.2005.00135.x

Angeli, C., & Valanides, N. (2009). Epistemological and methodological issues for the conceptualization, development, and assessment of ICT-TPCK: Advances in technological pedagogical content knowledge (TPCK). *Computers & Education, 52*(1), 154–168. doi:10.1016/j.compedu.2008.07.006

Council of Chief State School Officers Interstate Teacher Assessment and Support Consortium. (2013). InTASC model core teaching standards and learning progressions for teachers 1.0. https://ccsso.org/sites/default/files/2017-12/2013_INTASC_Learning_Progressions_for_Teachers.pdf

DeFauw, D.L. (2017). Writing with parents in response to picture book read alouds. *Reading Horizons: A Journal of Literacy and Language Arts, 56*(2), 22–51. http://scholarworks.wmich.edu/reading_horizons/vol56/iss2/3/

Foertsch, J., Moses, G., Strikwerda, J., & Litzkow, M. (2002). Reversing the lecture/homework paradigm using eTEACH web-based streaming video software. *Journal of Engineering Education, 6*(9), 267–274. doi:10.1002/j.2168-9830.2002.tb00703.x

Hussey, H.D., Fleck, B.K., & Richmond, A.S. (2014). Promoting active learning through a flipped course design. In J. Keengwe, G. Onchwari, & J. Oigara (Eds.), *Promoting active learning through the flipped classroom model* (pp. 23–46). IGI Global. doi:10.4018/978-1-4666-4987-3.ch002

Koehler, M.J., & Mishra, P. (2009). What is technological pedagogical content knowledge? *Contemporary Issues in Technology and Teacher Education, 9*(1), 60–70.

Mishra, P., & Koehler, M.J. (2006). Technological pedagogical content knowledge: A framework for teacher knowledge. *Teachers College Record, 108*(6), 1017–1054. doi:10.1111/j.1467-9620.2006.00684.x

Mishra, P. (2019). Considering contextual knowledge: The TPACK diagram gets an upgrade. *Journal of Digital Learning in Teacher Education, 35*(2), 76–78. doi:10.1080/21532974.2019.1588611

Pushor, D. (2015). Walking alongside: A pedagogy of working with parents and families in Canada. In L. Orland-Barak & C. Craig (Eds.), *International teacher education: Promising pedagogies (Part B)* (pp. 233–251). Emerald Group Publishing Limited.

Pushor, D., & Amendt, T. (2018). Leading an examination of beliefs and assumptions about parents. *School Leadership and Management, 38*(2), 1–20. doi:10.1080/13632434.2018.1439466

Reynolds, P.H. (2012). *Sky color*. Candlewick Press.

Shulman, L.S. (1986). Those who understand: Knowledge growth in teaching. *Educational Researcher, 15*(2), 4–14. doi:10.3102/0013189X015002004

Shulman, L.S. (1987). Knowledge and teaching: Foundations of the new reform. *Harvard Educational Review, 57*(1), 1–23. doi:10.17763/haer.57.1.j463w79r56455411

Shulman, L.S., & Shulman, J.H. (2004). How and what teachers learn: A shifting perspective. *Journal of Curriculum Studies, 36*(2), 257–271. doi:10.1177/0022057409189001-202

Thompson, A., & Mishra, P. (2007–2008). Breaking news: TPCK becomes TPACK!. *Journal of Computing in Teacher Education, 24*(2), 38–64.

Tondeur, J., van Braak, J., Sang, G., Voogt, J., Fisser, P., & Ottenbreit-Leftwich, A. (2012). Preparing pre-service teachers to integrate technology in education: A synthesis of qualitative evidence. *Computers & Education, 59*(1), 134–144. doi:10.1016/j.compedu.2011.10.009

Winkelmes, M.A., Bernacki, M., Butler, J., Zochowski, M., Golanics, J., & Weavil, K.H. (2016). A teaching intervention that increases underserved college students' success. *Peer Review: Emerging Trends and Key Debates in Undergraduate Education, 18*(1/2), 31–36. https://www.aacu.org/peerreview/2016/winter-spring/Winkelmes

Zurcher, M.A. (2016). Partnering with parents in the writing classroom. *The Reading Teacher, 69*(4), 367–376. doi:10.1002/trtr.1421

8 Transfer Writing Pedagogy
Becoming an Agent of Change in the Elementary Writing Classroom

Through the flipped writing methodology course's intricacies, preservice teachers are empowered to become agents of change in their future elementary classrooms as they develop their writerly voices, transfer pedagogical content knowledge of writing to teaching contexts, and begin to demonstrate teacher-writer characteristics that may or may not evolve into a teacher-writer identity. To support the grounded theory's conceptualization, in this chapter, I will discuss how participants demonstrate a "becoming" as a(n) writer, teacher of writing, teacher-writer, and agent of change. According to dictionary.com, becoming is defined as "any process of change … involving realization of potentialities, as a *movement* from the lower level of potentiality to the higher level of actuality." Movement is a key word in my mind. As Figure 0.1's gears move, as shown in the introduction, preservice teachers evolve through these "becomings" to teach writing effectively.

Becoming a Writer

Through our community of practice, writing workshop, preservice teachers demonstrate a becoming of writer stance as they make writerly choices to develop their writing abilities. These writing abilities support preservice teachers' writer identity. Their writer identity often needs to be strengthened because many preservice teachers reflect a distaste for writing due to past feedback or instruction. Preservice teachers who enjoy writing often have a natural disposition for writing or have experienced success with writing:

> Interestingly enough, even though I enjoy writing, particularly academically, I would not label myself as a writer. I do not write for pleasure, but I take pleasure in writing, as if that could possibly ever make sense.
> (Harper, Post-Course Interview, February 12, 2015)

Through our writing workshop experiences, I engage preservice teachers in writing instruction to help them develop a stronger appreciation for their individual voices. Through our writing community, preservice teachers meet, reconnect, or engage more fully with their inner writer.

> Every person wants their voice to be heard. Every single person wants to say something so finding the inner writer is basically pushing them into saying what they want to say even if they're afraid to say it.
> (Isla, Post-Course Interview, February 1, 2018)

To push preservice teachers to say what they want to say, I teach through mini lessons focused on their writerly needs. I demonstrate my own writing process and my choice to thread in snippets of my life's story across all genres. Sociocognitive apprenticeship (Englert et al., 2006) is evident in each mini lesson where I model with a think aloud (Atwell, 1998) and tackle writing's messiness to craft my voice through the writerly choices I make, similar choices preservice teachers make throughout the course. Choice gives rise to voice which gives rise to stories. Preservice teachers learn to thread their own stories and interests into narrative, informational/explanatory, and argument writing as Ryder's eportfolio quote illustrates:

> High school had conditioned me to hate writing essays. I'm glad to say that this class has turned that perception around for me quite a bit. All three of the essays in this class—personal narrative, informative, and argumentative—were enjoyable and never felt like a chore. It felt good to finally be able to write more than just five-paragraph argument essays about a topic I have no interest in. The essays had me employ skills I have used very rarely in the past for essay writing. I had to do actual research and planning for these essays. I actually felt true growth in my writing ability. It was an incredible feeling. Even if the essays didn't turn out the best or as I might've intended them to, I still can feel myself getting better at writing, a skill that is invaluable as a future teacher.

Preservice teachers need to develop their academic voices. Maybe within the next decade, preservice teachers will demonstrate a stronger orientation with the two prominent genres, informational/explanatory and argument, required by the Common Core State Standards (CCSS). As Shanahan (2015) detailed, the CCSS attempt to focus on argument writing more since "the Common Core emphasizes these three kinds of writing—summarization, analysis, and synthesis" (p. 471). Yes, students need to apply their reading comprehension skills and write arguments based on evidence they learn through text, but they also need to write their narratives.

Although I enjoy reading preservice teachers' three genre pieces, I especially enjoy the narratives they submit at the end of the semester. Preservice teachers complete their narratives outside of class following Phillips and Larson's (2015) "Becoming Writer" sections through their required reading. Heart-felt writing motivates writers to explore the writing process. Many teacher educators use, in part, poetry (e.g., Dymoke & Hughes, 2009), memoir (e.g., Martin & Dismuke, 2015), and narrative (e.g., Hawkins et al., 2019) to support preservice teachers' writing development, especially to combat ingrained negative writing perceptions.

Although all genres are important, like Araujo et al. (2014), I found preservice teachers have more experience with writing narratives than nonfiction writing. I focus the course's in-person writing workshop and academic service learning (ASL) content on nonfiction writing aligned with what the CCSS preservice teachers will teach their K-12 students. Shanahan (2015) stated:

> In the recent past, the writing skills most cherished and rewarded have been those that involved baring one's soul; with the Common Core it isn't self-revelation that is desired but the more public skills of note-taking, paraphrasing, summarization, deep reading, and critical response.
>
> (p. 476)

To become teachers of writing, preservice teachers must understand how to teach informational/explanatory, argument, and all other genres with the same passion they must teach narrative. Throughout the course experience and data, participants demonstrate a sense of promise, or vision to teach writing well (Parsons et al., 2017; Shulman & Shulman, 2004) as they first develop their writerly voices and then apply PCKW as teachers of writing.

Becoming a Teacher of Writing

Once preservice teachers experience writing workshop as writers, they need to experience teaching opportunities through authentic, real-world experiences (Herrington & Herrington, 2006) to apply the PCKW acquired throughout the course. Preservice teachers apply their learning through an afterschool writing clinic and the Young Authors' Festival (YAF). These authentic learning experiences create coherence between the PCKW preservice teachers learn in the course and apply in the field (Canrinus et al., 2019) through pedagogies of enactment:

> While teacher education is replete with examples of modeling, in which the teacher educator models classroom routines or activities for student

teachers, such approaches generally keep student teachers in the role of students. The move from discussing what one might do as a teacher to actually taking on the role of the teacher is a critical one, allowing novices to assume the role and persona of the teacher while receiving feedback on their early efforts to enact a practice.

(Grossman et al., 2009, p. 283)

The flipped writing methodology course's two ASL experiences are paramount to the preservice teachers' PCKW development and implementation as they learn to become teachers of writing. Stockinger (2007) stated, "University courses that embed authentic teaching in the field experience allow pre-service teachers to begin to develop a personal image of themselves as teachers" (p. 221). Through the afterschool writing clinic and YAF, preservice teachers develop confidence as they learn how to teach and evaluate elementary students' writing.

Prospective teachers increase their competence by applying content and pedagogical knowledge within authentic teaching contexts that include prolonged engagement and explicit guidance and mentoring; field experiences that support prospective teachers' differentiated instruction, including opportunities for one-to-one instruction (tutorial settings); and engagement with culturally and linguistically diverse students and families.

(ILA & NCTE, 2017, p. 5)

Preservice teachers apply PCKW learned throughout the course as evident in lesson plans with procedural steps including modeling, using mentor texts, writing authority lists, paraphrasing informational content, and connecting reading and writing instruction. Although direct transfer cannot be assumed from preservice teachers' oral or written comments, connecting their comments to their lesson plans reveals alignment.

Prominent across preservice teachers' lesson plans and reflections are preservice teachers' choices to model writing and build relationships. Granted, since Fall 2016, preservice teachers may use lesson plans I implement during our writing workshop sessions, but Harper created her own lesson plans during the Fall 2014 semester. Harper's first lesson plan's purpose stated, "To support student understanding of expository texts by modeling how to write an authority list and determine the audience for their future writing piece." Harper's lesson plans reveal her choice to implement course content related to modeling. Harper modeled her messy writing process for her student to teach that "it is okay to mess up." She and her student also used their authority lists to get to know one another. Harper admitted she "felt like [she] was lacking when teaching [her student] but [she] just needed to remember what [she] learned in class … and it brought her confidence back up" (Harper, Eportfolio, Fall 2014).

Modeling was prominent in other preservice teachers' instruction as well. Roberta noted in her field note journal that she used modeling to "scaffold her students' knowledge of various aspects of being an effective writer." Through her interactions with her students, she "learned from them what matters in teaching writing: That is repeated modeling, writing experiences, and conferencing." Sana stated in her eportfolio, "I learned modeling is a teacher's best friend when it comes to teaching. Modeling helps students learn better."

In addition to modeling, preservice teachers discovered elementary students often need support with motivation to select a writing topic and continue through the writing process. Annie discovered her student seemed unmotivated to select a topic from the authority list he created. Annie and her student "talked about the importance of picking a topic and sticking to it. They wrote a plan together and both signed it stating that the topic he chose was sports cars and that he would not change it again." In contemplating multiple ideas, the student moved forward with Annie's support. Similarly, Isla observed her student's motivational struggle but, like Annie, "refused to let his unmotivated phases stop [her] from allowing him to express his thoughts on paper."

Preservice teachers learn to support students' content development through reading and writing connections. Many elementary students choose topics from their authority lists they need to learn more about to write in the informational/explanatory genre. Thus, preservice teachers teach elementary students the Read, Reread, List, Compose (RRLC) strategy while students read books about their topic (Kettel & DeFauw, 2018). Jackie stated:

> I need to teach my kids to know their knowledge… You just have to read a lot of sources. And once you read a lot of sources and you have a good grip on your topic, I think it's easier then to go back and find important facts that you want to use or if you want to use direct quotes, but before finding those I feel like you have to understand what it is you're actually talking about. So, I was mostly just having [my students] focus on researching.
> (Jackie, Post-Course Interview, January 22, 2020)

Some preservice teachers also discovered tools their students needed that I did not provide through the course's content, such as using graphic organizers to support organization. Hawkins et al. (2019) teach preservice teachers to use graphic organizers, especially for crafting narrative arcs. Beginning

Fall 2020, I plan to provide a module on using graphic organizers to support writing development as Shannon found was needed per her field note journal reflection:

> The purpose of this session was to narrow down the topic, organize thoughts, and learn how to take information from articles without plagiarizing. For organizing thoughts, I used a backwards triangle with horizontal lines running through it. I had [my student] start off with a broad topic and narrow it down as the triangle got smaller ... From there, I had him use a graphic organizer to explain some details that he wanted to put into his article.

Once students select a narrow topic, preservice teachers find it easier to support their students' writing development. Annie reflected on one of her student's writing process in her field note journal reflection:

> Brainstorming about what cars he wanted to focus on, he created a list of about fifteen cars and the traits they had from memory! He then made a list of what information he wanted to add to his work and that list was also fifteen items long. I talked about how it might be difficult to get all of that information written in the time we had left and helped him pick four cars and four of the main topic ideas. He then asked if he could use my computer to go onto [his school's] website and look at the car book he liked. I asked him to show me what he meant and he took me to a site. He looked at how the pages of the car book were set up and said he wanted to do something like that. He named his work, and got a paragraph written. I am not sure where to find car books with the cars he wants in them. I looked in the library and couldn't find any. I am going to look in the lab before the clinic to see if I can find more mentor texts for him.

Annie experienced how writing often evolves naturally into reading, or vice versa, as students comprehend more content to include in their nonfiction writing pieces. Students also use books as mentor texts as Annie mentioned in her field note journal reflection about another student in her group:

> After finishing the book, I will model how I start setting up a writing piece in my journal. The first sentence is an interesting fact or an action happening. Last week when reading Cobras [my student] noticed that the book had chapters and decided that he wanted to write each page as a new chapter. So, I am going to find some books that have chapters to give an example of ways he could set the chapters up.

Ari connected reading and writing intricately, which demonstrated transfer from his reading methods course to the flipped writing methodology course. Per Ari's first lesson plan, he read aloud a biography about a musician from the local area and invited his student to complete a concept map. Following the read aloud, Ari's student did not list biography topics as writing interests, but science topics he wished to explore. Ari provided additional books with visuals and key vocabulary, all of which supported the writing process of the student, who was "given images of a plant's life cycle and asked to sort them in sequential order ... [and] a list of 3rd grade vocabulary words about a plant's life to explore and hopefully use in his story." The remaining lessons built on comprehending content to support writing development as Ari supported his student's sequencing, sentence structure, grammar, and revision. In the third lesson's reflection, Ari listed his student's typed sentences and the revised sentences per Ari's support. Ari stated in his field note journal reflection:

> The story is more condensed, coherent, and sequential when compared to [my student's] rough draft. Anything that was changed, altered, or omitted was at the discretion of [my student] and myself. Democratic judgments were made and [my student] had the final say on whether something should be changed. For next week, I wish to have [my student] cut out these sentences, put them in his book, and create illustrations.

Ari mentioned his student's motivation to complete the final copy in the blank book provided all writing clinic participants.

Preservice teachers welcome the opportunity to motivate student writing (Colby & Stapleton, 2006) through writing instruction, specifying writing strategies and language.

> During the course of the sessions, students were able to pick a topic to research; my students chose insects, cars, and snakes. As they researched their topics they began to use the writing strategies that I had been presenting in lessons prior, such as creating lists to narrow down their topic choices, freewriting to get the information on the page, and using mentor texts in order to organize their work.
> (Annie, Field Note Journal Reflection, Fall 2016)

Preservice teachers commended students for using writing strategies and spoke to students as writers. Roberta commented on how language plays a central role in supporting students' motivation to write: "If you want kids to see themselves as writers early on, you have to use writer's language with them, and encourage them to use writer's language as they talk about their peers' writings and their writings too" (Roberta, Post-Course Interview, February 9, 2017).

To support students' writing motivation, preservice teachers served as writing role models. Maceo, as evident in his first field note journal reflection, stated: "Next time, I should participate in the writing process with [my students] so they can see me work as well, which may motivate them to not complain about [writing]." I noted the following brief details about Maceo during Session 1 in my field notes walking between the three classrooms to observe:

- Does the coach have a name? Asking for more details.
- Observing lots of conversation to support writing development and idea generation.

These brief notes demonstrate some conversation evident in Maceo's first lesson implementation. Per my observations, Maceo did not model writing aside from showing the students his informational/explanatory piece. During Session 2, although not specified in his lesson plan, I observed Maceo writing with his students and I noted his following paraphrased quote: "We are almost done with our lists. Remember we have to write a couple of details about our topic. That's what I'm doing." Students often are motivated to write when they see their teachers write.

Preservice teachers need to teach as writing role models regardless of whether or not they see themselves as writers. Students perceive teachers who write as writers; thus, I require preservice teachers to write in a writer's notebook their (a) writing workshop pieces, (b) notes and try-it tasks from the modules, and (c) observations from the ASL experiences. Harper stated in her eportfolio she planned to use her writer's notebook "as a teaching and modeling tool in her future classroom that will show [her] students [she] too is a writer and [she] knows how hard and messy writing can be, but also how rewarding it can be." With a writer's notebook in hand, students likely will perceive their teachers as teacher-writers.

Becoming a Teacher-Writer

I address preservice teachers as teacher-writers and thread the teacher-writer terminology throughout the course (e.g., lesson plans, modules, readings, etc.) because I "deliberately support teachers in developing teacher-writer identities" (Whitney, 2017, p. 68). Despite my concerted efforts, only five preservice teachers used the term teacher-writer as detailed in this book's introduction. Jackie was the only participant who mentioned the term teacher-writer in her writing history essay which I used as a guide for the open-ended interview protocol; thus, I asked her about her teacher-writer perception:

It's definitely something I want to do. Like in my heart, I want to be a teacher-writer. And I'm pretty confident about what it means to be a teacher-writer after taking the class. I just think I need more experience to say like, yes, I'm definitely a teacher-writer. And I think there's some things that I need to work on, so that's why I'm kind of like probably.

(Jackie, Post-Course Interview, January 22, 2020)

Following Jackie's interview, I sent all participants an anonymous five-item Qualtrics survey with one Likert-scale item and four short-response items, because I wanted to know if their teacher-writer identity changed post-course:

1. In your own words, define what it means to be a teacher-writer.
2. Are you a teacher-writer? (Definitely/Probably Yes, Might or Might Not, Probably/Definitely No)
3. Explain why you do or do not identify as a teacher-writer.
4. What do teacher-writers do?
5. Do you enjoy teaching writing? Why or why not?

Four participants (15%) submitted surveys, certainly a low percentage. Interestingly, three participants marked "definitely yes" and one participant marked "probably yes" to the prompt: Are you a teacher-writer? Obviously, more research is needed to study teacher-writer identity in preservice, student, and inservice teachers, but the participants' quotes align with teacher-writer definitions and instruction (Whitney et al., 2014). The final bullets in the following two lists are from the participant who marked "probably yes" to being a teacher-writer. Participants defined teacher-writers as educators who:

- "are pro writing and enforce the love for writing in all subjects",
- "share their writing with their students, and expose students to authentic writing experiences",
- "come across writer's block ... and address potential blocks students may face during their own writing," and
- "act as a role model for different ways of writing."

According to these four participants, teacher-writers:

- "instill in all their students that they are capable of writing and are good at it",
- "teach students strategies that strengthen the way they communicate through writing",
- "find and use texts ... with authors who use words and phrases to inspire students to use the same phrasing in their writing," and

- "teach their students through example and model how to do different types of writing."

Throughout the course, I help preservice teachers enact teacher-writer skillsets such as creating authentic writing in front of the students, modeling writing strategies, connecting writing and teaching experiences, and choosing publication opportunities (Whitney, 2017). Through my teaching, I demonstrate teacher-writer strategies because I choose, personally and professionally, to live a teacher-writer's life. I know "I can respond to student writers—to both their writing and the *person* writing—from an empathetic stance" (Whitney, 2017, p. 71) due to my teacher-writer identity.

Although many preservice teachers demonstrate teacher-writer characteristics or aspirations, the preservice teachers who may have been in the initial stages of teacher self-identification (Stockinger, 2007), still step away from a teacher-writer identification. Before preservice teachers identify as teacher-writers, they need to take developmental steps to achieve the teacher-writer identity. Preservice teachers, especially, may need more time to self-identify as teacher-writers, particularly since Collier and her team (2015) found student teachers self-identified as teachers of writing, not teacher-writers: "Clearly, writing is not only a mechanical process but is also deeply connected to the internal construction of one's identity as a writer, and to the social construct of one's identity as a future educator" (p. 96).

Self-identification as a teacher-writer may not be necessary (Brooks, 2007). I conducted a previous study of a fourth-grade teacher who implemented effective writing pedagogy and acted as a teacher-writer (DeFauw, 2016). Although the fourth-grade teacher did not self-identify as a teacher-writer, her students identified her as a teacher-writer. Through this flipped writing methodology course, preservice teachers applied PCKW but did so without identifying specifically as teachers or writers. I still believe preservice teachers need to self-identify as teacher-writers so they enact a writerly life for themselves and their future students even though my own research has shown that self-identification as a teacher-writer may not be necessary (DeFauw, 2016). More research needs to be conducted. What is *necessary* is that students see their teachers as teacher-writers. What is *ideal* is preservice teachers, at least eventually, self-identify as teacher-writers so they may be agents of change in their classrooms, schools, districts, states, and nations.

Becoming an Agent of Change

As teacher educators, we must empower preservice teachers to be agents of change in the classroom, but such change begins with educator preparation institutions requiring at least one writing methodology course for preservice teachers. The National Commission on Writing (2003) stressed the need for required writing methodology courses almost two decades ago, but few universities require such courses (Brenner & McQuirk, 2019; Myers et al., 2016). Myers et al. (2019) and Sanders et al. (in press) studied 15 teacher educators who focused on the writing process and provided experiential learning opportunities in local schools for preservice teachers to apply PCKW through their educator preparation program's writing methodology course. This line of research is moving us, as a field, in the right direction to impact policy (Myers et al., 2016, 2019; Sanders et al., in press).

Research shows teachers' experiences with writing pedagogy impact their instruction. "Lived experiences, where preservice teachers are immersed as student-participants of pedagogical practice, affected preservice teachers' efficacy and perceptions of their preparedness to teach writing" (Pytash et al., 2015, p. 151). Everitt (2012) discovered preservice and student teachers' efficacy, per 49 candidates she followed from coursework through student teaching, is impacted by field experiences, school and district support, colleagues/peers feedback, and coursework/assignments.

> Prospective teachers use what they have learned during their literacy teacher preparation course work when teaching in pre-K-12 field placements, and later in their own classrooms, and they teach with competence.
> (ILA & NCTE, 2017, p. 5)

To become agents of change in the classroom, preservice teachers must first be empowered with high-quality writing instruction that guides them in developing as teachers of writing and hopefully as teacher-writers.

Preservice teachers enrolled in the flipped writing methodology course engage in a community of practice tasked with educator responsibility. Preservice teachers synergize their individual and communal understanding of writing to facilitate their students' learning through the ASL opportunities. Shulman and Shulman (2004) stated, "An accomplished teacher is a member of a professional community who is ready, willing, and able to teach and to learn from his or her teaching experiences" (p. 259). Granted, across their educator preparation program of study, preservice teachers vary regarding their development of "the features of ... teacher learning: Vision, Motivation, Understanding, Practice, Reflection, and Community" (Shulman & Shulman, 2004, p. 259). Vision is evident in preservice teachers' motivation to apply what they have learned not only within the ASL experiences, but in the future as inservice teachers. I am not certain Shulman and Shulman (2004) began the feature list with vision and motivation purposefully, but connecting their conceptual framework for teacher learning and development with my own grounded theory, I argue motivation and vision must propel preservice teachers into their first few years of teaching.

Beginning teachers need to implement PCKW to support elementary students' writing development through the writing process. Preservice teachers need such experiences to help them navigate the tensions they likely will experience in teaching.

Reaching through Tension

Regardless of the vision preservice teachers may bring to the classroom, tension is inherent in their educational contexts, evident in student teaching experiences. For example, Annie shared tension she felt during her student teaching experience with a student who experienced trauma. Tentative to permit sharing, Annie struggled with the tension of understanding sharing as an important component to the writing process and protecting her student:

> A negative experience. It's a little confidential, but like one of the kids … you don't know what's going to come out in their writing. Sometimes more personal stuff comes out in their writing. And they will just air out their dirty laundry in front of kids and you don't really want the rest of the kids or anyone who comes in to hear that … So, I guess like making sure what they're going to share is appropriate because sometimes it slips through the cracks and you're like ugh they shouldn't have said that.
> (Annie, Post-Student Teaching Interview, February 20, 2018)

Carly faced tension in her student teaching experience related to topic choice and modeling. Carly encouraged a student's topic choice about video games, which did not align with her mentor teacher's approved topics for students to explore in their writing. "He wanted to talk about … what he did and how he played [video games] with his brother. And he just wrote a whole story about that, which made him really motivated to write." (Carly, Post-Student Teaching Interview, December 14, 2015). Also, Carly faced tension between her choice to model writing for her students and her cooperating teacher's perception that modeling permitted copying:

> I'm a big advocate of modeling … and she kind of was a little hesitant about it. She was like, I don't like to model for everything, because then they just copy me. And I kept thinking in my head, what's wrong with that? What's wrong with them, you know, well, maybe not copying you with the same topic. But copying you means that they understood that modeling and that it worked, and that they're able to apply it to their own writing.
> (Carly, Post-Student Teaching Interview, December 14, 2015)

As a long-term substitute teacher following her student teaching experience in the same classroom, Annie experienced tension with implementing writing workshop the way she envisioned. Annie promoted freewriting with her second-grade students, a writing strategy used throughout the course, but she struggled with implementing writing workshop to focus on different genres within units of study:

> I have trouble introducing new genres of writing. I think that professional development is needed for not explaining but giving examples on exciting ways to get them involved and to get them ready for, you know, different types of groups, different types of writing, that they're going to be faced with in their school careers and just their lives. It's not really structured. They're still just getting used to the writing. But I'm just having more structure in my writing lessons. More structure.

As this quote demonstrates, Annie is cognizant of the tension she experiences with providing her second-grade students more structure through a writing workshop framework. She encourages freewriting for self-expression, especially since she has students who have experienced trauma and she wants her students to benefit from the healing aspects writing may provide. Yet, she is not teaching her second-grade students to choose writing topics within genres. She is still learning to orchestrate writing workshop components and use mentor texts to introduce genre structures.

Riddled with a negative connotation, the word tension does not promote preservice teachers' vision of instruction. Telling preservice teachers they will experience tension as inservice teachers does not promote their vision. Even vision can create tension. "Vision can make some teachers' ambitions soar, but it can also prompt self-doubt and despair" (Hammerness, 2001, p. 144). Tension creates stress. Tension blocks opportunities. Tension traps teachers into teaching like their apprenticeship experiences have solidified (Lortie, 1975). Yet, the positive denotation of tension means stretching or straining. I prefer the word stretching, because stretching requires reaching. Preservice teachers may be empowered to reach through the tension (Hammerness, 2001) so they hold their vision, notice the tension, reach through the tension, and act, implementing effective writing instruction for all elementary students, within all contexts.

References

Araujo, J., Szabo, S., Raine, L., & Wickstrom, C. (2014). Bridging the stories of experience: Preservice teachers revise their thinking about writing and the teaching of writing in an undergraduate literacy course. In S. Vasinda, S. Szabo, & R. Johnson (Eds.), *37th yearbook of the Association of Literacy Educators and Researchers* (pp. 225–238). Association of Literacy Educators and Researchers.

Atwell, N. (1998). *In the middle: New understandings about writing, reading, and learning*. Boynton/Cook Publishers, Inc.

Brenner, D., & McQuirk, A. (2019). A snapshot of writing in elementary teacher preparation programs. *The New Educator*, *15*(1), 18–29. doi:10.1080/1547688X.2018.1427291

Brooks, G.W. (2007). Teachers as readers and writers and as teachers of reading and writing. *Journal of Educational Research*, *100*(3), 177–191. doi:10.3200/JOER.100.3.177-191

Canrinus, E.T., Klette, K., & Hammerness, K. (2019). Diversity in coherence: Strengths and opportunities of three programs. *Journal of Teacher Education*, *70*(3), 192–205. doi:10.1177/0022487117737305

Colby, S.A., & Stapleton, J.N. (2006). Preservice teachers teach writing: Implications for teacher educators. *Reading Research and Instruction*, *45*(4), 353–376. doi:10.1080/19388070609558455

Collier, S.M., Scheld, S., Barnard, I., & Stallcup, J. (2015). The negotiation and development of writing teacher identities in elementary education. *Teaching/Writing: The Journal of Writing Teacher Education*, *4*(2), 90–112. http://scholarworks.wmich.edu/wte/vol4/iss2/6/

DeFauw, D.L. (2016). Fourth-grade students' perceptions of their teacher as a writer. *Michigan Reading Journal*, *48*(3), 7–16.

Dymoke, S., & Hughes, J. (2009). Using a poetry wiki: How can the medium support pre-service teachers of English in their professional learning about writing poetry and teaching poetry writing in a digital age. *English Teaching: Practice and Critique*, *8*(3), 91–106.

Englert, C.S., Mariage, T.V., & Dunsmore, K. (2006). Tenets of sociocultural theory in writing instruction research. In C.A. MacArthur, S. Graham, & J. Fitzgerald (Eds.), *Handbook of writing research* (pp. 208–221). The Guilford Press.

Everitt, J.G. (2012). Teacher education and accountability: Adapting to prospective work environments in public schools. In S. Kelly (Ed.), *Assessing teacher quality: Understanding teacher effects on instruction and achievement* (pp. 137–159). Teachers College Press.

Grossman, P., Hammerness, K., & McDonald, M. (2009). Redefining teaching, re-imagining teacher education. *Teachers and Teaching: Theory and Practice*, *15*(2), 273–289. doi:10.1080/13540600902875340

Hammerness, K. (2001). Teachers' visions: The role of personal ideals in school reform. *Journal of Educational Change*, *2*(2), 143–163. doi: 10.1023/A:1017961615264

Hawkins, L.K., Martin, N.M., & Cooper, J. (2019). Preparing elementary writing teachers: An inquiry-driven, field-based approach to instruction. *Teaching/Writing: The Journal of Writing Teacher Education*, *6*(1), 132–160. https://scholarworks.wmich.edu/wte/vol6/iss1/8

Herrington, A., & Herrington, J. (2006). What is an authentic learning environment. In A. Herrington & J. Herrington (Eds.), *Authentic learning environments in higher education* (pp. 1–14). Information Science Publishing.

International Literacy Association (ILA) and National Council of Teachers of English (NCTE). (2017). *Literacy teacher preparation [Research advisory]*. https://www.literacyworldwide.org/docs/default-source/where-we-stand/ila-ncte-teacher-prep-advisory.pdf

Kettel, R.P., & DeFauw, D.L. (2018). Paraphrase without plagiarism: Use RRLC (Read, Reread, List, Compose). *The Reading Teacher*, *72*(2), 245–255. doi:10.1002/trtr.1697

Lortie, D.C. (1975). *Schoolteacher: A sociological study*. University of Chicago Press. https://www.press.uchicago.edu/ucp/books/book/chicago/S/bo3645184.html

Martin, S.D., & Dismuke, S. (2015). Teacher candidates' perceptions of their learning and engagement in a writing methods course. *Teaching and Teacher Education*, *46*, 104–114. doi:10.1016/j.tate.2014.11.002

Myers, J., Scales, R.Q., Grisham, D.L., Wolsey, T.D., Dismuke, S., Smetana, L., Yoder, K.K., Ikpeze, C., Ganske, K., & Martin, S. (2016). What about writing? A national exploratory study of writing instruction in teacher preparation programs. *Literacy Research and Instruction*, *55*(4), 309–330. doi:10.1080/19388071.2016.1198442

Myers, J., Sanders, J., Ikpeze, C.H., Yoder, K.K., Scales, R.Q., Tracy, K.N., Smetana, L., & Grisham, D.L. (2019). Exploring connections between writing methods teacher education courses and K-12 field experience. *Action in Teacher Education*, *41*(4), 344–360. doi:10.1080/01626620.2019.1600600

National Commission on Writing. (2003). *The neglected "R": The need for a writing revolution*. http://www.vantage.com/pdfs/neglectedr.pdf

Parsons, S.A., Vaughn, M., Malloy, J.A., & Pierczynski, M. (2017). The development of teachers' visions from preservice into their first years teaching: A longitudinal study. *Teaching and Teacher Education*, *64*, 12–25. doi:10.1016/j.tate.2017.01.018

Phillips, D.K., & Larson, M.L. (2015). *Becoming a teacher of writing in elementary classrooms*. Routledge.

Pytash, K.E., Testa, E., & Nigh, J. (2015). Writing the world: Preservice teachers' perceptions of 21st century writing instruction. *Teaching/Writing: The Journal of Writing Teacher Education*, *4*(1), 142–163. https://scholarworks.wmich.edu/wte/vol4/iss1/8/

Sanders, J., Myers, J., Ikpeze, C., Scales, R., Tracy, K., Yoder, K.K., Smetana, L., & Grisham, D. (in press). A curriculum model for K-12 writing teacher education. *Research in the Teaching of English*.

Shanahan, T. (2015). Common Core State Standards: A new role for writing. *The Elementary School Journal*, *115*(4), 464–479. doi:10.1086/681130

Shulman, L.S., & Shulman, J.H. (2004). How and what teachers learn: A shifting perspective. *Journal of Curriculum Studies*, *36*(2), 257–271. doi:10.1177/0022057409189001-202

Stockinger, P.C. (2007). Living in, learning from, looking back, breaking through in the English language arts methods course: A case study of two preservice teachers. *English Education*, *39*(3), 201–225.

Whitney, A. (2017). Developing the teacher-writer in professional development. In T. Cremin & T. Locke (Eds.), *Writer identity and the teaching and learning of writing* (pp. 67–80). Routledge. doi:10.4324/9781315669373

Whitney, A.E., Zuidema, L.A., & Fredricksen, J.E. (2014). Understanding teachers' writing: Authority in talk and texts. *Teachers and Teaching: Theory and Practice*, *20*(1), 59–73. doi:10.1080/13540602.2013.848515

Conclusion
Teach Writing

> Much like a cross section of an ancient tree, writers have rings on their insides. These tiny imprints tell the story of writers' experiences and environment. Each ring reveals their history, their deep knowing from their first encounters with words until their most recent writing experiences ... all of these experiences leave behind a ring.
>
> (Anderson, 2011, p. 241)

I want to help preservice teachers grow to be the kind of teachers who "facilitate the formation of those rings, and the rings that follow [that] will forever be affected" (Anderson, 2011, p. 242).

Preservice teachers need to learn to partner with families, the *teachers* who form those first rings and flow through all the others; colleagues, the known and unknown *teachers* they collaborate with along each writer's journey, growing a new ring each academic year; and authors, the *teachers* who seep throughout those rings. All of these *teachers* create the sociocultural roots from which students develop as writers.

Through the flipped writing methodology course, I strive to facilitate preservice teachers' *becomings* to connect with students' root systems through their teaching and to grow as educators. Fitting many puzzle pieces of writing pedagogical content knowledge of writing (PCKW) into a semester-long course, I ensure in-person time provides authentic learning opportunities for preservice teachers to apply PCKW. Per curricular-design requirements, preservice teachers participate in writing workshop to develop as writers, tutor elementary students to develop as teachers of writing, and acquire PCKW in-person and virtually that they apply through academic service learning (ASL) opportunities to transfer to their future teaching experiences.

To build preservice teachers' confidence in writing, teacher educators need to teach PCKW within a community of practice to ensure a curricular impact for preservice teachers and their future elementary students (Shulman & Shulman, 2004). Writing community is built through relationships with students, families, teachers, and published children's book authors. I choose to use flipped learning to manage time efficiently so preservice teachers experience a writing community as a writer and as a teacher to promote transfer of PCKW to their future classrooms. Although Shulman (1987) coined the term pedagogical content knowledge, four years prior, Graves (1983) defined this concept for writing:

> The teaching of writing demands the control of two crafts, teaching and writing. They can neither be avoided, nor separated. The writer who knows the craft of writing can't walk into a room and work with students unless there is some understanding of the craft of teaching. Neither can teachers who have not wrestled with writing, effectively teach the writer's craft.
>
> (pp. 5–6)

Although cognizant that some teachers teach writing well without being writers themselves (e.g., Brooks, 2007), I agree with Graves (1983). I wonder what the rings on the inside of me and every teacher reveal about our writerly stories. I wonder what our students' rings reveal about us and how we fit together the puzzle pieces of instruction into a coherent curriculum.

Piecing Together the Curricular Puzzle

I piece together curricular content that my experiences, research, and reading have taught me can be applied directly to the elementary classroom. The hats I have worn—third-grade teacher and literacy coach—are layered within the hats I wear now—teacher educator and researcher. The adage that there exists a gap between college and K-12 classrooms can be lessened through the choices teacher educators make to use pedagogy we know transfers directly to the K-12 classroom. Transfer transparency is inherent in my teaching. As I teach, I am transparent with how I expect preservice teachers to apply teaching strategies and content to the classroom. I think aloud about the decisions I make as I teach to help preservice teachers reflect upon how their experiences as students in the course should transfer to their future teaching contexts as preservice and inservice teachers.

Throughout this book, I highlight course requirements for preservice teachers. Some of the assignments align with those Scales et al. (2019) detail, focused on supporting preservice teachers' development as writers and as teachers of writing. Like Scales et al. (2019), I share their goal to "broaden ideas of how to help candidates develop as writers and as teachers of writing" (p. 78). Granted, there are innumerable ways to teach our writing methodology courses, but we must come to some kind of consensus of what preservice teachers need in order to be prepared to teach writing for K-6 students.

Sanders et al. (in press) provide a beehive diagram of a K-12 writing curriculum model for teacher educators to use; the diagram's hexagonal shapes puzzle together to form a beehive. Each hexagonal shape includes an instructional goal or a curriculum component (e.g., assessment, writing process, field experiences, etc.). Graham and Harris (2015) stated, "With CCSS, writing is now central to the mission of schooling" (p. 459) for K-12, but writing also needs to be a central component of elementary teacher preparation programs. Using a coherent curriculum, teacher educators need to support preservice teachers' continued application of PCKW through varied experiences.

In summarizing the Pedagogical Content Knowledge (PCK) (Shulman, 1986, 1987) and Pedagogical Content Knowing (PCKg) (Cochran et al., 1993) research, Angeli and Valanides (2009) stated, "Prospective or even beginning teachers have incomplete and superficial levels of PCK ... their PCK continually grows with new experiences related to teaching and learning" (p. 156). Teacher educators need to teach a writing curriculum enriched with field experiences to support transfer of learning from a required writing methodology course for preservice teachers to their student teaching and inservice teaching contexts (Myers et al., 2016; Myers et al., 2019; Sanders et al., in press). If our elementary students are provided with writing instruction from teachers who feel confident in their own ability to teach writing, the students will experience academic success. Elementary students' success is strengthened when preservice teachers' preparation is strengthened.

As teacher educators, we envision facilitating preservice teachers' development to become high-quality writing teachers. Yet, there is tension evident for so many of us as we try to ensure preservice teachers are well-prepared to teach writing, yet we battle to do so within universities that will not require such a course. We must reach through this tension with our shared voices and act. No longer can we just say writing is important and needs to be taught. We need to be proactive. We need to teach. We need to help create policies that require writing methodology courses for preservice teachers. We need to do our part to ensure elementary students are provided with the strongest foundation of writing instruction possible. Teacher educators need to help preservice teachers roll from one experience to another as the gears depicted in Figure 0.1 (see Introduction) rotate, move, and propel each preservice teacher into the profession.

The Grounded Theory's Gears

Pictured in my mind, the gears in Figure 0.1 move: making writerly choices, identifying as teacher-writers, and transferring as evidence. The making writerly choices gear moves fastest because it has fewer teeth and has to keep up with the transferring as evidence gear. The data show preservice teachers' writerly choices coincide with transfer to the ASL contexts. For example, preservice teachers desire free choice for writing topics and, in most cases, students' topic choices move the writing process forward during the writing clinic. Also, connected to the making writerly choices gear is the identifying as a teacher-writer gear which rotates in the opposite direction. This rotation or movement connects to Ivanič's (1998) view of seeing identification as a verb, or as something that is evolving and taking shape. Preservice teachers engage in "identity *work*," experience to experience, context to context (Ivanič, 2006, p. 21) as they grow to identify as a writer, as a teacher of writing, and as a teacher-writer.

Each gear moves at a different rate, the teeth sliding quickly or slowly into the next openings, but regardless of the speed, there's still movement. The teacher-writer identity gear may move slowly while preservice teachers are grasping all they must learn regarding PCKW, but within the writing community, they are making writerly choices and transferring their experiences to their teaching contexts during the semester and beyond. Except for Roberta and Jackie, the data show preservice teachers more than likely did not identify yet as teacher-writers. Without the required writing course, they would not have an opportunity to put the gears together to begin the "identity *work*" necessary to evolve from identities as writers to teachers of writing to teacher-writers (Ivanič, 2006, p. 21).

In the gear trio, the transferring as evidence gear moves slower yet with more force and that force propels preservice teachers into vision for their future teaching experiences as inservice teachers. "Visions focus on what teachers hope to instill in students" (Parsons et al., 2017, p. 12). Preservice teachers envision high-quality writing instruction for their future elementary students as the following quotes illustrate:

> I can hardly wait to have my own classroom to implement the teaching strategies, as well as the experiences I gained from the service-learning projects, in order for my future students to view writing as a reflective and enjoyable process.
> (Harper, EPortfolio, Fall 2014)

> One of my professional goals, as a result of this course, is to include as much family support in my classroom as I can, especially when it comes to writing.
> (Carly, EPortfolio, Fall 2014)

> The big lesson I learned [from the Young Authors' Festival] was that there are so many ways for students to express themselves and learn at the same time, and that is an extremely crucial part of education. I will definitely remember that lesson for my entire teaching career.
> (Ryder, EPortfolio, Fall 2016)

> The importance of this course was the hands-on experiences I participated in. These hands-on experiences helped me visualize myself as a teacher. Before the writing clinic, I had zero knowledge of planning and

teaching a writing workshop lesson, but this experience was very beneficial for me to use all my experiences as a teacher.

(Sana, EPortfolio, Fall 2019)

Throughout the course experiences and data, participants demonstrate a vision or promise to teach writing well (Parsons et al., 2017; Shulman & Shulman, 2004). Like a puzzle, the gears fit together and propel preservice teachers into their professional identities as teachers of writing and hopefully some day as teacher-writers.

Recently, my daughter Dayana brought home Cale Atkinson's picture book *Where Oliver Fits*, published by Tundra Books. As we enjoyed the book which details Oliver's experience as a round puzzle piece and his battle to fit in with the other puzzle pieces, I kept thinking about the connections the picture book has with my experience in designing the writing course. *Where Oliver Fits* sounds a bit like *where all of it fits*, and as a teacher-educator, I often question where all of the PCKW fits into a single course. Tension is evident in scarce time—always. Yet, I choose to reach through the tension and teach within the set boundaries, choosing to do as much as I can within my circle of influence. I think about how my experience fits into the literature, and how all of us, as teacher educators, teach our courses effectively although differently. It would be interesting to pursue research in which we observe teacher educators in action, in-person and online, as our colleagues teach the many pieces of PCKW so we can continue to learn from each other (Scales et al., 2019).

And so that 1,000-piece puzzle that emptied into my hands almost a decade ago, continues to grow, evolve, and fit together just right to help me grow as a teacher-writer educator. Every day, I aim to be a stronger teacher educator tomorrow than I am today, and I hope I am stronger today than I was yesterday. I must continue to grow to pass my understanding of PCKW to preservice teachers who, in collaboration with families and published children's book authors and illustrators, will support many elementary students' writing development now and in the future. I trust this book has demonstrated clearly how I have learned to teach preservice teachers to provide high-quality writing instruction at this point in my career. Yet, even this book's content, even my own current understanding provides only a glimpse into the puzzle I still feel I am learning how to fit together, piece by piece.

References

Atkinson, C. (2017). *Where Oliver fits*. Tundra Books.
Anderson, J. (2011). *10 things every writer needs to know*. Stenhouse Publishers.
Angeli, C., & Valanides, N. (2009). Epistemological and methodological issues for the conceptualization, development, and assessment of ICT-TPCK: Advances in technological pedagogical content knowledge (TPCK). *Computers and Education*, *52*(1), 154–168. doi:10.1016/j.compedu.2008.07.006

Brooks, G.W. (2007). Teachers as readers and writers and as teachers of reading and writing. *Journal of Educational Research, 100*(3), 177–191. doi: 10.3200/JOER.100.3.177-191

Cochran, K.F., DeRuiter, J.A., & King, R.A. (1993). Pedagogical content knowing: An integrative model for teacher preparation. *Journal of Teacher Education, 44*(4), 263–272.

Graham, S., & Harris, K.R. (2015). Common Core State Standards and writing: Introduction to the special issue. *The Elementary School Journal, 115*(4), 457–563. doi:10.1086/681963

Graves, D.H. (1983). *Writing: Teachers & children at work.* Heinemann.

Ivanič, R. (1998). *Writing and identity: The discoursal construction of identity in academic writing.* John Benjamins Publishing Company

Ivanič, R. (2006). Language learning and identification. In R. Kiely, P. Rea-Dickens, H. Woodfield, & G. Clibbon (Eds.), *Language, culture and identity in applied linguistics* (pp. 7–29). Equinox Publishing.

Myers, J., Scales, R.Q., Grisham, D.L., Wolsey, T.D., Dismuke, S., Smetana, L., Yoder, K.K., Ikpeze, C., Ganske, K.,& Martin, S. (2016). What about writing? A national exploratory study of writing instruction in teacher preparation programs. *Literacy Research and Instruction, 55*(4), 309–330. doi:10.1080/19388071.2016.1198442

Myers, J., Sanders, J., Ikpeze, C.H., Yoder, K.K., Scales, R.Q., Tracy, K.N., Smetana, L., & Grisham, D.L. (2019). Exploring connections between writing methods teacher education courses and K-12 field experience. *Action in Teacher Education, 41*(4), 344–360. doi:10.1080/01626620.2019.1600600

Parsons, S.A., Vaughn, M., Malloy, J.A., & Pierczynski, M. (2017). The development of teachers' visions from preservice into their first years teaching: A longitudinal study. *Teaching and Teacher Education, 64,* 12–25. doi:10.1016/j.tate.2017.01.018

Sanders, J., Myers, J., Ikpeze, C., Scales, R., Tracy, K., Yoder, K.K., ... Grisham, D. (in press). A curriculum model for K-12 writing teacher education. *Research in the Teaching of English.*

Scales, R.Q., Tracy, K.N., Myers, J., Smetana, L., Grisham, D.L., Ikpeze, C., Yoder, K.K., & Sanders, J. (2019). A national study of exemplary writing methods instructors' course assignments. *Literacy Research and Instruction, 58*(2), 67–83. doi:10.1080/19388071.2019.1575496

Shulman, L.S. (1986). Those who understand: Knowledge growth in teaching. *Educational Researcher, 15*(2), 4–14. doi:10.2307/1175860

Shulman, L.S. (1987). Knowledge and teaching: Foundations of the new reform. *Harvard Educational Review, 57*(1), 1–22. doi:10.17763/haer.57.1.j463w79r56455411

Shulman, L.S., & Shulman, J.H. (2004). How and what teachers learn: A shifting perspective. *Journal of Curriculum Studies, 36*(2), 257–271. doi:10.1177/0022057409189001-202

Appendix: Course Components

The Appendix details course components. Table A.1 provides a syllabus example followed by Table A.2, which lists course assignments. Next, the online module's screencast topics and formative assessments that I call try-it tasks are detailed. Some module content is available at my website, http://danielledefauw.com/. Table A.3 provides mini lesson topics and resources used in-person. Some mini lessons are provided as examples of in-person writing workshop lessons on my website.

Flipped Learning Screencast Topics and Try-it Tasks for Writer's Notebook

Teacher-Writers

- Select one writing prompt from Slide 9 (e.g., childhood map, photos, songs, etc.) or another prompt of your choice and write.
- Quickwrite for five minutes to a prompt on slide 11 (e.g., one word, emotion, objects, sentence stems, etc.).

Writing Workshop Framework

- Describe your experiences with how you have been taught to write. Note if you have or have not experienced writing workshop. Share your thoughts.
- I recommend in the lecture that writing workshop is often quiet time. Consider your own writing process and how you use conversation to support your writing. Think about how you would allow for conversation and quiet writing time during the same writing workshop. What is your preference as a teacher-writer and as a student?

Table A.1 Syllabus Example with In-Person Tasks, Online Modules, Required Readings, and Assignments

Session	In-Person	Online	Reading	Assignment
1	Writing Community ASL Writer's Notebooks Peer Feedback Form PLCs	Module 1: Teacher-Writers & Writing Workshop	Phillips & Larson (2015): Preface	
2	Create, compose, and revise explanatory/informative writing. PLC: YAF			Writing History Essay
3	Compose, revise, and edit explanatory/informative writing using mentor texts PLC: YAF	Module 2 Conferencing & Nonfiction	Phillips & Larson (2015): Becoming Writer Getting Started, pp. 3–4; Ch. 1 Gaillet & Eble (2016): Ch. 1	
4	Compose, revise, and edit explanatory/informative writing for academic purposes and audiences. PLC: YAF			
5	Revise and use explanatory/informative writing rubric. PLC: YAF	Module 3 Revision vs. Editing & CCSS	Phillips & Larson (2015): Ch. 2 Gaillet & Eble (2016): Ch. 2	YAF Blurb
6	Use research skills to cite sources correctly. PLC: YAF			
7	Create, compose, and revise argument writing. PLC: YAF	Module 4 Assessment & Argument	Phillips & Larson (2015): Ch. 3; Gaillet & Eble (2016): Chs. 3–4	Explanatory/Informative Writing Peer Feedback

(Continued)

Appendix 141

Table A.1 Continued

Session	In-Person	Online	Reading	Assignment
8	Compose, revise, and edit argument writing using mentor texts. PLC: YAF			
9	Compose, revise, and edit argument writing for academic purposes and audiences. PLC: YAF	Module 5 Publication & Citing & RRLC	Phillips & Larson (2015): Part II, pp. 55–56; Ch. 4; Gaillet & Eble (2016): Chs. 9–10	
10	Choose an argument topic and publication opportunity. PLC: YAF			Explanatory/ Informative Writing
11	Revise and use argument writing rubric. PLC: YAF	Module 6 ELL Writers & Authentic Writing	Phillips & Larson (2015): Ch. 5; Gaillet & Eble (2016): Ch. 12	Writer's Notebooks with Try-It Tasks for Modules 1–5 Argument Writing Bibliography
12	Compose and revise argument writing. PLC: Writing Contest Evaluation	Module 7 Unmotivated Writers & Grammar	Phillips & Larson (2015): Ch. 6	
13	Compose and revise argument writing. PLC: Writing Contest Evaluation			
14	Compose and revise argument writing. PLC: Writing Contest Evaluation	Module 8 Interactive Writing & Handwriting	Phillips & Larson (2015): Ch. 7; Becoming Writer pp. 4–10	Argument Writing Outline
15	Compose and revise argument writing. PLC: Writing Contest Evaluation			
16	Create, compose, and revise narrative writing. PLC: YAF	Module 9 Writing Clinic & YAF	Phillips & Larson (2015): Ch. 8; Becoming Writer pp. 57–60 and pp. 107–112	Argument Writing Peer Feedback
17	Compose, revise, and edit narrative writing analyzing mentor texts. PLC: YAF Debrief			

(Continued)

142 Appendix

Table A.1 Continued

Session	In-Person	Online	Reading	Assignment
18	Compose, revise, and edit narrative writing for personal purposes and audiences; choose a topic and publication opportunity.			Argument Writing Piece
19	Using Flipped Learning Components PLC: Create Family Resources	Module 10 Fiction & Show Me/Don't Tell Me	Review Writing Clinic Module	
20	PLC: Create Family Resources			
21	Writing Clinic Session 1	Module 11 Parent-Writers & Flipped Learning	Phillips & Larson (2015): Ch. 9; Becoming Writer pp. 175–178	Virtual Family Resource
22	Writing Clinic Session 2			Narrative Writing Feedback
23	Writing Clinic Session 3		Phillips & Larson (2015): Ch. 10	Writer's Notebooks with Try-It Tasks for Modules 6–11
24	Writing Clinic Session 4			Narrative Writing
25	Writing Clinic Session 5			Field Note Journal
26	Writing Clinic Celebration			Argument Writing Presentation and Revision
No Final Exam				MPortfolio Reflection

Note: Academic Service Learning (ASL); Common Core State Standards (CCSS); Professional Learning Communities (PLC); Read, Reread, List, Compose (RRLC); and Young Authors' Festival (YAF).

Table A.2 Flipped Writing Methodology Course Assignments

Required Assignments	Description
Writing history essay	Detail your history as a writer for personal and professional purposes, positive and negative experiences with writing, easy and difficult steps about writing, personal and professional goals for writing, and future visions for using writing throughout your career.
Writer's notebook entries	Complete outside-of-class and in-class writing requirements in your writer's notebook.
Narrative piece	Choose a personal narrative topic and audience. Use writer's craft to detail your experience.
Informational/Explanatory piece	Choose a topic you want to teach third- through fifth-grade students and write like the picture book authors we study.
Argument piece with publication opportunity	Identify an authentic publication opportunity in order to write for a specified audience. Revise thoroughly, synthesize research that is appropriately cited, argue/explain, and prepare for publication.
Peer feedback	Provide and receive pre-submission peer feedback for each genre piece to support the revision process.
Young Authors' Festival parent session	Partnerships design a 10-minute session to engage the parents at the YAF.
Flipped family resource	Flip the YAF parent session content; create a screencast and provide electronic resources for families to use at home.
Field note journal entries	Use your field note journal to track lesson plans, observations, and reflections before, during, and after your tutoring of one or more writing-clinic students.
EPortfolio reflection	Reflect upon the component(s) of the ASL projects and/or course experiences that supported your growth as a writer and/or teacher.
Modules	Complete one online module weekly for ten weeks.

The Heart of Writing Workshop: The Writing Conference

- Imagine you are interviewed for a teaching position in which you would be required to use writing workshop. Respond to this question: Why do you conference with students about their writing and how will you organize your conferencing during writing workshop?
- What do you find challenging about conferencing with students and how would you work through the challenge(s)?

Teaching the Writing Details: Nonfiction

- Describe mentor texts.
- How will you use mentor texts as a writer and as a teacher-writer?

Revision

- Write a 3, 2, 1; include three details of what you learned, two challenges, and one question. Feel free to adjust the 3, 2, and 1. For example, if you have more questions than challenges, you'll select three questions, two details you learned, and one challenge.
- Elementary students often do not want to revise. When they're done, they believe they're done. How would you support 30 students' revision processes?

Revising versus Editing

- What are the differences between revising and editing, and how would you teach students the differences?
- If you see a student editing when he/she should be revising, how would you intervene?

Common Core State Standards (CCSS)

- How would you ensure you teach the writing CCSS?
- What do you like and dislike about the English Language Arts CCSS?

Assessing Writing

- High-stakes writing assessment is a reality in education. How would you prepare your students for high-stakes writing assessment?
- How would you collect data about your students' writing, and how would you use the data to inform your instruction?

Argument Writing

- When teaching argument, we begin with opinion, then persuasive, and then argument writing. Describe each of these genres and how they are different and how they are alike.
- How do audience and purpose play into argument writing?

Publication Opportunities

- What roles do audience and purpose play in a writer's experiences?
- How would you support your students' publication processes and opportunities?

Use Research Skills to Cite Sources Professionally

- Why is it important to cite sources appropriately?
- Describe how you would teach K-6 students differently concerning the level of detail you would require they include in their sources and citations.

RRLC: Read, Reread, List, Compose

- Describe your experience using the RRLC strategy as a writer and as a teacher-writer (Kettel & DeFauw, 2018).
- How would you teach students the differences between paraphrasing and summarizing?

Supporting ELL Writers

- How do you feel about teaching ELL writers?
- Imagine a principal provides the following interview prompt: Tell me three strategies you plan to use with ELL writers. How would you respond?

Authentic Writing

- Consider your own experiences with learning. Detail an authentic learning experience you've had at any point in your life. How did this learning process feel?
- Write about how you would make a specific lesson you have in mind more authentic.

The Art of Supporting Unmotivated Writers

- Write a journal response or reflection about a time you felt you could not learn to do something, such as writing, cooking, sports, dancing, teaching, etc.
- Write a journal response about a student you have taught or you are teaching who struggles with writing. Describe strategies you intend to

use, or wish you would have known to use to support them. Describe your emotions toward this student.

Embedding Grammar Instruction in Writing Workshop

- Notice and name the instructional opportunities within the mentor text sentences.
- Write sentences like those the mentor text shows and how I model (dash, interrupter pattern, serial pattern, closer pattern, opener sentence, etc.) (Anderson, 2005).

Interactive Writing

- Notice and name what you observe through the first-grade interactive writing lesson. Reflect on the teacher's instruction and what you would do similarly or differently and why.
- Define shared and interactive writing. How are they different? How are they similar?
- Define and provide examples of phonological awareness, phonemic awareness, and phonics.

Handwriting

- Describe your own experiences with handwriting instruction as a student, adult, and teacher.
- Imagine you are an early elementary teacher facilitating parent/teacher conferences. How would you respond to the following parent's comment and question: I am concerned about my child's handwriting. What can I do to help them write neater?

Writing Clinic

- As you plan to teach writing to elementary students, what do you feel nervous or excited about?
- If a parent or principal asked you the purpose of the writing clinic and what you plan to do during the session, how would you respond?

Young Authors' Festival

- How would you include published children's book authors and illustrators in your writing workshop community?
- Describe your experience(s) with author visits or writing festivals as a student and teacher.

Teaching the Writing Details: Fiction

- Notice and name the instructional opportunities within the mentor text sentences.
- How are mentor texts beneficial and challenging in a writing workshop community? How would you work through the challenges?
- How would you couple reading and writing workshop?
- Why do students need to read the genre before they write the genre?

Show Me, Don't Tell Me

- How would you model Show Me, Don't Tell Me as a teacher-writer?
- Describe the specific types of writer's craft that writers may use to show versus tell.

Supporting Parent-Writers

- How can families support their children's writing development?
- How would you support parents regarding writing instruction?

Table A.3 Flipped Writing Methodology Course Sample Lessons and Mentor Texts

Session	Mini Lesson Topic	Mentor Texts
1	Idea generation through childhood maps (Frank, 2003)	Baylor, B. (1991). *Your own best secret place*. Atheneum Books. Juster, N. (2005). *The hello, goodbye window*. Hyperion Books. Leedy, L. (2000). *Mapping Penny's world*. Henry Holt & Co.
2	Writing leads and endings	Numerous picture books
3	Explode a moment	Frazee, M. (2003). *Roller coaster*. Harcourt, Inc.
4	Use dialogue and other writer's craft	Scieszka, J. (2008). *Knucklehead: tall tales & mostly true stories about growing up Scieszka*. Viking.
5	Generate nonfiction authority lists (Atwell, 1998)	Frazee, M. (2006). *Walk on! A guide for babies of all ages*. Harcourt, Inc. Numerous nonfiction books
7	Craft sentences	Jenkins, M. (2001). *Chameleons are cool*. Candlewick Press.
8	Publish	Peruse publication opportunities' requirements

Flip Your Writing Workshop

- Write a letter to yourself listing the top ten details you've learned through flipped learning that you do not want to forget concerning how to teach writing.
- What are the benefits and challenges of flipped learning and how do you plan to work through the challenges?

References

Anderson, J. (2005). *Mechanically inclined: Building grammar, usage, and style into writer's workshop*. Stenhouse Publishers.

Atwell, N. (1998). *In the middle: New understandings about writing, reading, and learning*. Boynton/Cook Publishers, Inc.

Frank, C.R. (2003). Mapping our stories: Teachers' reflections on themselves as writers. *Language Arts, 80*(3), 185–195.

Gaillet, L.L., & Eble, M.F. (2016). *Primary research and writing: People, places, and spaces*. Routledge.

Kettel, R.P., & DeFauw, D.L. (2018). Paraphrase without plagiarism: Use RRLC (Read, Reread, List, Compose). *The Reading Teacher, 72*(2), 245–255. doi: 10.1002/trtr.1697

Phillips, D.K., & Larson, M.L. (2015). *Becoming a teacher of writing in elementary classrooms*. Routledge.

Index

Page numbers in **bold** indicate tables. Page numbers in *italics* indicate figures.

academic service learning (ASL): 15, 25, **26–27**, 121, 128, **142**; objectives for 38; preparation for, 44, 70; preservice teachers' perceptions of 40, 42; *see also* writing clinic; writing contest; Young Authors' Festival
Again! (Gravett) **74**
agent of change 118, 127–130; *see also* identity
Akiko [Series] (Crilley) 83
Anderson, J. 133, 146
anecdotes 57, 66
apprenticeship 1, 130; sociocognitive 22, 119
argument: mentor texts of 50; modeling 25, 56–57; module content 44, **143**, 144; standards and 38; teaching 24, 66; writing 49, 52; *see also* genre
Arnoldo, M. **74**
ASK program *see* Authors, Specialists, Knowledge program
ASL *see* academic service learning
assessment: course evaluation **41**; data category 8, **9**; formative for preservice teacher learning 42, 139, **140–142**, 144; writing contest and 15, 44
assignments 40, 42, 54, 107, 113; bias in 115; descriptions of 83, **143**; lists of **140–142**; transfer through 128, 134; transparently designed 112
Atkinson, C. 137

audience: assignments and **140–142**, **143**; choice of 28, 49, 50, 55–56, 58, 121; data subcategory **9**; motivation and 48; objectives and 37; purpose and 10, 13, 48; 53, 54, 144–145; writing celebration and 79; writing contests and 94, 100, 101
authenticity 2, 145; audience and 53–54; choice and 14; context and 14–15, 39, 81–82; course and 83, 120–121, 133; objectives and 37; products and 10, 39, 106; purpose and 22–23, 49; writing contests and 94, 96, 99–100; writing workshop and 49, 89, 127; authority 54
authority lists 11, 44, 121–122, **147**; flipped family resource topics 111
authors *see* children's book authors
Authors, Specialists, Knowledge program 88–89
author visits 83, 89–90, 146
axial coding 8, 10

Baylor, B. **147**
biases 68; awareness of 12–13, 14, 114–115
Bolts, M. **74**
Bradley, D. 30, 79
brainstorming 11, 68, 123
bread winner, The (Ellis) 88–89
Brody's ghost [Series] (Crilley) 83
Bud, not Buddy (Curtis) 83
Bunting, E. **74**
Buzzeo, T. 29, 82, 89, 90

Index

Canvas *see* learning management system
celebration 90; skill-development through 67; writing clinic 10–11, 31, 66, 78–79
challenges: formative assessment topics as 143, 144, 147, 148; inservice teachers and 2; interview questions and 5; parent-writers and 109, 110; preservice teachers and 48, 53, 54; teacher-writers and 12, 54 93; writing clinic and 28, 29, 66, 69, 72
Chameleons are cool (Jenkins) 147
children's book authors 4, 9, 49–50, **74–75**; ASK program and 89, 90; celebrate with 15; connect families with 66, 81, 89, 90; contest winners 92–93; preservice teacher as 11, 55, 68; writing clinic and 79; Young Authors' Festival and 29; 32, 146
choice 11, 46, 48, 119; attitudes to writing 52; data category 8, **9**; motivation and 56–57; teaching and 134; topic 129; word 45, 51, 67; *see also* audience; flipped learning; themes
coach 68, 134
coding 8, **9**, 10, 13
Cohn, A. **74**
collaboration: peer 39, 106, 137; writing clinic and 70, 71; Young Authors' Festival and 69, 70
colored car, The (Elster) 83
colour of home, The (Hoffman) **74**
Coming on home (Woodson) 50
Common Core State Standards 38, 49, 66, 119–120, 135, **140**, 144
communities of practice 22–23, 49, 118, 128, 133; *see also* professional learning communities
conferencing: course description and 30, 38; data subcategory **9**; module content and 44, **140–142**, 143; preservice teacher to student 87, 122; virtual, 5, 40, 56; writing workshop and 4, 28, 48, 52, 53, 78
confidence: lack of 52, 57; preservice teachers 42, 45, 121, 122, 145; student 29, 31

constant comparative method (CCM) of analysis 8
conventions *see* grammar
conversation: modules and 139; negative 40, flipped family resource topics 111; promoting 111, 112; teaching and 125; writing contest and 98
Council for the Accreditation of Educational Professionals (CAEP) 36
course: children's literature **84**; *see also* flipped course
craft *see* writer's craft
Crilley, M. 83
Curtis, C. P. 30, 83

day you begin, The (Woodson) **75**
data: analyses 8, 10; coding **9**; collection 111; schedule **6–7**; sources 5
Dear Juno (Pak) **74**
debrief 29, **141**
demonstrations *see* modeling
dialogue 51–52, **147**
dialogue journal *see* family dialogue journal
Dig, wait, listen: A desert toad's tale (Sayre) 50
discussion 3, 10, 40, 42
drafting 4, 22, 49, 52; preservice teachers' perceptions of 51, 57, 124

editing 4; 37, 49, 90; data and 67; revision vs. 52, **140**, 144
Ellis, D. 88–89
Elster, J. A. 32, 83
English Language Learners 145
ethnicity: of author 115; of preservice teachers **6–7**; of writing clinic participants **26–27**, 28, 30–31, 69
evaluations: course **41**
explanatory writing *see* nonfiction writing

family dialogue journal 73, 76, 111
family involvement: flipped family resource 31–32, 111, 115, **142**, **143**; parent-writers **73**; writing clinic 31, **88**; Young Authors' Festival 81, 105
family-school partnerships *see* home/school partnerships

Index

Faulkner, M. 29, 31, 79, 82, 83
feedback: data sources 5; data subcategory **9**; distant audience and 100; family 78, 114; peer 50, 52; sharing and 53; from teacher educator 23, 42, 52, 106; writer development and 57, 118, 121, 128
fiction writing 147; ASK program and 88; as genre 86; mentor texts and 29; writing clinic and 10, 66; writing contests and 95
field experience 13, 28, 38; conflict and 8; literature and 21, 24–25, 39, 121, 128, 135; preservice teachers' perceptions of 9; *see also* flipped family resource; writing clinic; writing contest; Young Author's Festival
Firsts (Cohn) 74
flipped course **140–142**; components of 43–44; **140–142**, **143**, **147**; design of 3, 15, 22, 43; examples of 23–25; in-person sessions **140–142**; objectives of 36–38; organization of **84**; progression of 25, **26–27**, 28, 31–32; reading within **140–142**; required 4; questions guiding research 4–5, 48, 54–55, 105; time distribution **26–27**, 39; *see also* flipped learning; modules; screencasts
flipped family resource 84, 106–107, 111–112; assignment description of 107, **143**; examples of 108–109; progression of **84**; reflections of 114–115; resources for 110; *see also* posters
flipped learning 14–15, 22, 23, 28; 38, 46; choice to use 38–40; definition of 3; interview questions and 5; students' creation of 105; students' perceptions of 42–43, 112–113; theoretical framework of 23; *see also* flipped family resource
focus lessons *see* lesson plans
focus of book 14–15
Frazee, M. **147**
freewriting: families and 73, 108, 110; flipped family resource topics 111; modeling 56–57, **73**, 108, 109–110;

preservice teachers and 124, 130; published authors' use of 44
funds of knowledge 78, 89

general education 30, 37
genre 30, 38, 39, 49, 119; ASK program and 89; choice and 10; features of 54, 130; modeling use of 51, 119; objectives and 38, 49, 119, 120; revision of 52; teaching 50, 51, 54, 130; transfer writing skills across 29, 54, 67; writing contests and 96; *see also* argument; narrative; nonfiction writing; poetry
Giff, P. R. 89
Google suite 46, 106, 107, 110–111
grading 98; writing contest entries 96, 97
grammar 24; module content **141**, 146; teaching 124
Grandma's records (Velasquez) **75**
graphic organizers: data and 67–68, 122; module content 69, 123
Gravett, E. **74**
grounded theory 4, *13*, 14, 15; catalyst for 22; discussion of 118, 128–129, 135–136; limitations of 14; methodology of 5, 8, 10, 13
Groundhog's dilemma (Remenar) 31, 83
guided writing *see* interactive writing

Hagen, C. 82
handwriting: dictation and 1; module content **141**, 146; preservice teachers and 52–53
hello, goodbye window, The (Juster) **147**
Hest, A. **74**
Hoffman, M. **74**
home/school partnerships: developing 15, 115; family dialogue journals and 76; flipped family resource and 107, 112; parent sessions as 28, 29, 73, 81; writing contests and 94, 101

ideas: data and 67; generating 11, 24, 67, **88**, **147**; graphic organizers for 68; objectives and 37; publishing 48; sharing 31, 70; writing clinic and generating 122, 123, 125

identity: data category 8, **9**; identifying as verb 136; interview questions and 5; objectives and 37; professional learning communities 39; questions guiding research 4, 5, 48, 54–55; teachers as writers 23; teachers of writing 137; teacher-writers 9, 11–14, 54–55, 58, 118, 125–127; writer 92, 118
ILA *see* International Literacy Association
imitation *see* modeling
informational/explanatory writing *see* nonfiction writing
inservice teachers: ASK programs as 88; author visits and 89–90; data subcategory **9**; enrollment with 27–29, 69; flipped learning use as 109, 110, 113; observations of 5, **6–7**, 7–8; questions guiding research 5, 105; professional development for 25; self-efficacy as 106; teacher-writer identities as 12, 54, 126; tension for 130; transfer of learning as 32, 43, 128, 134, 135, 136; unprepared to teach writing 13; writing events implemented as 88
InTASC *see* Interstate Teacher Assessment and Support Consortium
interaction *see* family involvement
interactive writing: module content **141**, 146
International Literacy Association (ILA) 22, 36, 43, 108, 121, 128
International Reading Association (IRA) 77
Interstate Teacher Assessment and Support Consortium (InTASC) 36, 114
interview 3, 5, 8, 125; analysing 42, 112; ASK program and 88–89; limitations and 14; member checking and 10; module content 143, 145; participants' **6–7**, 14
Ivanič, R. 55, 136

Jenkins, M. **147**
Juster, N. **147**

Kiss good night (Hest) **74**

Knucklehead: Tall tales & mostly true stories about growing up Scieszka (Scieszka) **147**

learning management system 3, 8, 22, 39, 44, 45–46, 49
Leedy, L. **147**
lesson plans 8, 39, **143**, **147**; challenges with 40, 130; choosing mentor texts **147**; family 88; flipped 45, 46, 113; mini 4, 28, 39, 44, 48, 50–52, **88**; mentor texts for 101, **147**; modeling through 51, 65, 78, 119, 125; module content 145, 146; read aloud 83; revision 51, 57; objectives for 38; transfer and 121, 124, 125, 137; writing clinic 5, 11, 66–67, 68, 69; Young Authors' Festival 11, 85, 86
Little brothers & little sisters (Arnoldo) **74**
Lloyd-Jones, S. 48
LMS *see* learning management system
Look! I wrote a book! (And you can too!) (Lloyd-Jones) 48
Lord, C. 89
Lovell, P. **74**

Mack, J. **74**
Mapping Penny's world (Leedy) **147**
memory string, The (Bunting) **74**
memos 8, 14, 44, 45
mentor texts: challenges with 130; choosing 48; data and 67; definition of 11, 50; examples of 51, **147**; family resources as 29, 108, 109; module content **140–141**, 144, 146, 147; nonfiction 66; objectives and 30, 38; teacher-writers' writing as 11, 50, 65, 78; winning contest entries as 94, 99, 100–101; writing clinic and 121, 123, 124; writing workshop and 4, 28, 45, 50; Young Authors' Festival and 86–87, 121
Michigan Student Test of Education Progress (MSTEP) 99
Miki Falls [Series] (Crilley) 83
mini lessons *see* lesson plans
modeling 2, 4; argument 25, 56–57; authors 90; conferencing and 53; course description and 25, 30, 38;

families and 73, 78, 88, 108, 114; flipped family resource topic 111; flipped learning 45; freewriting 56–57, **73**, 108, 109–110; genre 51, 119; grading 97; graphic organizers 67–68; importance of 9; lesson plans and 51, 65, 78, 119, 125; module content 146, 147; revision 51; teacher influence and 56–57, 120; teacher-writers 65, 126–127; technology 52, 106, 109, 110; tension in 129; writing clinic 11, 55, 121–122, 123, 125; writing workshop 23, 25, 28, 45, 48–50; Young Authors' Festival 11, 86–87, 121; *see also* notice and name; think aloud
modules: assessment in 42; components of 43–44, **140–142**; monitoring completion of 44; schedule of **140–142**
motivation: data category 8, **9**; preservice teachers' 57, 128; supporting writers' 122, 124, 145–146; writing contests and 94, 100
MSTEP *see* Michigan Student Test of Education Progress
My heart fills with happiness (Smith) **75**
My name is Yoon (Recorvits) **75**

NAEP *see* National Assessment of Educational Progress
narrative 28, 38, 44, 49, 66, 119–120, **143**; arc 122; audience for 55–56; course description and 30, 38; as mentor text 50, 66; module content **141–142**; writing contest and 96; *see also* genre
National Assessment of Educational Progress (NAEP) 21
National Council of Teachers of English (NCTE) 22, 36, 43, 108, 121, 128
National Writing Project (NWP): course objectives 37; tenets of 4, 22
NCTE *see* National Council of Teachers of English
night Henry Ford met Santa, The (Hagen) 82
nonfiction writing: ASK program and 88; course and 66, 120; informational/explanatory writing 25, 38, 52, 122; mentor texts and 29, 66; module content 144; unit of study 28; writing clinic and 10, 11, 30, 31, 65, 66, 79, 123; *see also* argument; genre
notebooks *see* family dialogue journals; writer's notebook
note taking 42, 44, 120
notice and name 45, 112 123, 146, 147
Not 'til tomorrow, Phoebe (Zwilich) **75**
novice teachers *see* preservice teachers
NWP *see* National Writing Project

Observations 5, **6–7**, 14, 24, 40, 125
One cool friend (Buzzeo) 29, 82
organization: of book 14–15; of course 22, 24–25; 49, 54, **84**, **140–142**, 143
Owl moon (Yolen) **75**

pacing: course 39, 40, **82**, **84**, **140–142**
Pak, S. **74**
paraphrasing *see* read, reread, list, compose (RRLC)
parent-writer 55; module content 142, 147; prompts **74–75**; sessions 69, 73; steps **73**, 108, 109; Young Authors' Festival **82**
PCK *see* pedagogical content knowledge (PCK)
PCKW *see* pedagogical content knowledge of writing (PCKW)
pedagogical content knowing (PCKg) 3, 135
pedagogical content knowledge (PCK) 3, 32, 106, 135
pedagogical content knowledge of writing (PCKW) 22, 134; course development 3–4, 25, 28, 36, 43, 128, 133–134; inservice teachers and 13, 129; modeling 45; questions guiding research 4, 82, 105; teachers of writing and 120, 121; teacher-writer identity and 13, 127; tension and 137; transfer of 8–9, 11, 14, 22, 109, 121, 136; writing clinic and 29, 65, 120
Pictures of Hollis Woods (Giff) 101
PLC *see* professional learning communities
poetry 28, 97, 100, 120
Polacco, P. **74**
posters **27**, 31, 81, **82**, 83, 84, 115

preservice teachers: academic service learning experiences 3–4, 25; challenges 48, 53, 54; as children's book author 11, 55, 68; confidence 42, 45, 121, 122, 145; ethnicity of **6–7**; formative assessment of 42, 139, **140–142**, 144; interviews **6–7**; learning of pedagogical content knowledge of writing *13*, 21–22; motivation and 57, 128; perceptions of parent-writers 76, 77; perceptions of writing clinic 40, 42, 51, 77; perceptions of writing contest 98; perceptions of Young Authors' Festival 42, 84, 86–87, 90, 136–137; published 12, 42, 55, 57–58; requirements 49, 83, 107; *see also* themes
prewriting 4, 37, 49
process approach *see* writing process
professional learning communities (PLC) 3, 15, 39, 41, **140–142**
prompts: for parent-writers 73, **74–75**, 76, 108, 110; for preservice teachers 49, 126, 139, 145; writing contests 92, 94, 96, 99–100; *see also* try-it tasks
publish 49, 145; children's book 48; course objectives 37; inservice teachers 28; preservice teachers 12, 42, 55, 57–58; teacher-writers 12; writing contest entries 29, 97, 101; writing workshop 4, **147**
purpose: authentic 22, 94, 100, 101; choices as 10, 48, 50; course 32, 38; data subcategory **9**; evaluative 94, 100; in-person sessions' **140–142**; flipped family resource 107; lesson plan's 121; module content 144–145, 146; motivation 128; professional writing 2, 30; teacher-writers' 54; writing clinic 123

quick-writing *see* freewriting
quiet place, The (Stewart) 73, 83

reaching 129, 130, 135, 137
read alouds: children's literature course 83; parent-writer sessions 73, 76, 108, 109–110; writing celebration 28, 31, 78; writing clinic 68, 124; writing contest 81, 98–99; Young Authors' Festival 30, 87
read, reread, list, compose (RRLC) 145; data and 67; paraphrasing 67
readwritethink.org 108
Recorvits, H. **75**
Relatives Came, The (Rylant) 50
Remenar, K. 31, 83
revision 22, 51–52; assignments 143; authors' 30, 93; course and module content 44, **140–142**, 144; course objectives and 37; data and 67; preservice teachers' 52, 57; students' 124
Reynolds, P. H. 108, 109
Rollercoaster (Frazee) **147**
Roll of thunder, hear my cry (Taylor) 93
RRLC *see* read, reread, list, compose
rubrics **140–142**; for writing contests 29, 96–97
Rules (Lord) 89
Rumford, J. **75**
Rylant, C. 50

Sayre, A.P. 45, 50
SCBWI *see* Society of Children's Book Writers and Illustrators
scheduling 4, **6–7**, 65, 69–70, **82**, **88**; challenges with 30, 40
Schmidt, G. D. 83
Scieszka, J. **147**
screencasts 43–44; topics 139, **140–142**, 143–148
selective coding 10, 13
self-efficacy 23, 29, 106
service-learning *see* academic service learning
sharing writing 4, 22–23, 48; tension and 129
Silent music: A story of Baghdad (Rumford) **75**
Sky color (Reynolds) 108, 109
small brown dog with a wet pink nose, A (Stuve-Bodeen) **75**
Smith, M.G. **75**
Society of Children's Book Writers and Illustrators (SCBWI) 92
Sociocultural 4, 22, 133
Song of the trees (Taylor) 93

Soto, G. **75**
Standardized assessment: data subcategory **9**; Michigan Student Test of Education Progress (MSTEP) 99; writing contest preparation for 94, 99–100
Standards 36–38
Stand tall, Molly Lou (Lovell) **74**
Stewart, S. 73, 83
Stuve-Bodeen, S. **75**

Taylor, M. D. 93, 94
teacher candidates *see* preservice teachers
teacher education: challenge for 120, 127; transfer to contexts 45, 46, 120, 134; writing methodology course in 36, 38, 135, 137
teachers of writing 23, 32; becoming 120–121, 133, 136, 137
teacher-writer: becoming 118, 125–127, 128, 136, 137; bias as 23, 49, 56; data category, 8, **9**; developing as 54–55, 58; identifying as 8, **9**, 11–12, 135, 136; module content 44, 139, **140**, 144; questions guiding research 4, 48, 54–55; writing workshop and 28; Young Authors' Festival and 86; *see also* transfer
technological pedagogical content knowledge (TPACK) 105–106, 107; information and communication technology and (ICT-TPCK) 106
technology: access to 112, 113; data and 67; model with 106, 109; reflections 43, 111; *see also* flipped course; flipped family resource; Google suite; screencasts
tension 129, 130, 135, 137
texts *see* mentor texts; fiction writing; genre
Thank you, Mr. Falker (Polacco) **74**
themes *13*; identifying as teacher-writer, 8, **9**, 11–12, 135, 136; making writerly choices, 8, **9**, 10, 135–136; transferring as evidence and vision, 8–9, **9**, 111, 135, 136
things I can do, The (Mack) **74**
think aloud 4, 22–23, 28, 97, 119, 134
Those shoes (Bolts) **74**

Too many tamales (Soto) **75**
TPACK *see* technological pedagogical content knowledge
transfer 32; data category 8, **9**; as evident and vision 8–9, **9**, 111, 135, 136; home/school contexts 73, 114; limitations 14, 121; questions guiding research 4–5, 82; teacher-writers 23, 58; transparency 134; *see also* pedagogical content knowledge of writing
try-it tasks 139, **140–142**, 143–148
Turtle, turtle, watch out! (Sayre) 50
tutor 4, 38, 42, 66, 133, **143**

university writing clinic *see* writing clinic

Velasquez, E. **75**
video lectures *see* screencasts
vision *13*, 128–129, 130; transferring as evidence and 8, **9**, 11, 111–112, 120, 136–137
vocabulary 51, 124
voice 51; development of 2, 4, 23, 55, 57–58, 118–119; published author 50; teacher-writer 12, 15, 22; writing contests and 94

Walk on! A guide for babies of all ages (Frazee) **147**
Watsons go to Birmingham–1963, The (Curtis) 83
Wednesday wars, The (Schmidt) 83
Where Oliver fits (Atkinson) 137
Woodson, J. 50, **75**
workshop *see* writing workshop
writer 4, 22; author visits and 90; becoming 118–120, 136; data subcategory **9**; identity as 12; interview as 5; making writerly choices, 8, **9**, 10, 135–136
writer's craft 134, **147**; data of 67; developing 54; flipped content 45; mentor texts and 51; module content 45, 147; narrative and **143**, **147**; students and 49; writing clinic and 29; writing contests and 94, 101
writer's notebook 52, 125, **140–142**, **143**; modeling with 68; for students 72, 81, 90

writing assessments *see* assessments
writing clinic 4, 15, 69; celebration of 10–11, 29, 31, 66–67, 78–79; challenges 28, 29, 66, 69, 72; choice within 10, 136; content of 66; data subcategory **9**; interview questions and 5; lesson plans for 5, 11, 66–67, 68, 69; modeling 5, 11, 66–67, 68, 69; module content 146; nonfiction writing 10, 11, 30, 31, 65, 66, 79, 123; participants **26–27**, 28, 30–31, 69, 71; pedagogical content knowledge of writing 29, 65, 120; preparation for 28, 44, 65; preservice teachers' perceptions of 40, 42, 51, 77; program vignette 65; progression of 69, 70–71; questions guiding research 4, 82, 105; resources for 10, 124; schedule **6–7**, 25, 39, 65, **88**, **142**; steps 71–72, 73; students' perceptions of 70; transfer through 11, 28, 43, 55, 67, 120–121, 137; transfer to 87, 101

writing contest 4, 92–93; authentic learning opportunities as 94, 96; benefits of 94; drawbacks of 96; entries **26–27**; evaluation process 5, 97–98; interview questions and 5; implementation process 96; as mentor texts 100–101; prizes and 99; program vignette 81; questions guiding research 4; rubric, 96; scheduling **140–142**; standardized assessment preparation through 94, 99–100

writing methodology course *see* flipped course

writing process 4, 22–23; author visits and the 89; course objectives and 30, 36–37, 38; data subcategory **9**; flipped family resource topic 114; as recursive 48; module content 44; as social 53; *see also* writing clinic

writing rubric *see* assessments; rubric
writing teachers *see* teachers of writing; teacher-writers
writing workshop 3–4, 22–23, 25, 48–49; as authentic 49, 89, 127; catch and release 53; conferencing and 4, 28, 48, 52, 53, 78; developing teacher-writer identities through 54–55; mentor texts and 4, 28, 45, 50, **147**; modeling within 11, 23, 25, 28, 45, 49–50; module content 44, 139, 148; questions guiding research 4, 48; participation in 49; as social 53; teacher-writer identity development through 4, 54

Yolen, J. 75
Young Authors' Festival (YAF) 4, 40, 81, 82, 83, 84; as academic service learning opportunity 81, 87; breakout sessions at **6–7**, 30, **82**, **84**, **85**; children's book authors 29; 32, 146; data subcategory **9**; family involvement 81, 105; interview questions and 5; lesson plans and 11, 85, 86; mentor texts and 86–87, 121; modeling 11, 86–87, 121; module content 44, 146; preparation for 44; preservice teachers' perceptions of 42, 84, 86–87, 90, 136–137; program vignette 81; progression of 28–29, 30, 31–32, 82; questions guiding research 4, 38, 82; schedule 39, **82**; **140–141**; steps 87–88; transfer through 86–87, 120; *see also* flipped family resource; preservice teachers; writing contest

Your own best secret place (Baylor) **147**

Zwillich, J. 75

For Product Safety Concerns and Information please contact our EU
representative GPSR@taylorandfrancis.com
Taylor & Francis Verlag GmbH, Kaufingerstraße 24, 80331 München, Germany

www.ingramcontent.com/pod-product-compliance
Lightning Source LLC
Chambersburg PA
CBHW051747230426
43670CB00012B/2197